The Coerced Conscience

The Coerced Conscience examines liberty of conscience, the freedom to live one's life in accordance with the dictates of conscience, especially in religion. It offers a new perspective on the politics of conscience through the eyes of some of its most influential advocates and critics in Western history: John Milton, Thomas Hobbes, Baruch Spinoza, and Pierre Bayle. By tracing how these four philosophers, revolutionaries, and heretics envisioned, defended, and condemned this crucial freedom, Amy Gais argues that liberty of conscience has a more controversial history than we often acknowledge today. Rather than defend or condemn a static, monolithic view of liberty conscience, these figures disagreed profoundly on what protecting this fundamental principle entails in practice, as well as the extent of the threat of hypocrisy and conformity to freedom. This revisionist account of liberty of conscience challenges our intuitions about what it means to be free today.

AMY GAIS is a Lecturer in the Department of Political Science and the Interdisciplinary Project in the Humanities at Washington University in St. Louis. She is a political theorist specializing in freedom, specifically the question of how individuals resist oppression. She was the recipient of the Robert C. Wood Prize and an American Council of Learned Societies Emerging Voices finalist. Her work has been published by *Political Theory*, *Review of Politics*, and *History of European Ideas*, as well as public-facing outlets, such as *Inside Higher Ed*.

The Coerced Conscience

AMY GAIS
Washington University in St. Louis

CAMBRIDGE
UNIVERSITY PRESS

Shaftesbury Road, Cambridge CB2 8EA, United Kingdom

One Liberty Plaza, 20th Floor, New York, NY 10006, USA

477 Williamstown Road, Port Melbourne, VIC 3207, Australia

314–321, 3rd Floor, Plot 3, Splendor Forum, Jasola District Centre, New Delhi – 110025, India

103 Penang Road, #05–06/07, Visioncrest Commercial, Singapore 238467

Cambridge University Press is part of Cambridge University Press & Assessment, a department of the University of Cambridge.

We share the University's mission to contribute to society through the pursuit of education, learning and research at the highest international levels of excellence.

www.cambridge.org
Information on this title: www.cambridge.org/9781009372008
DOI: 10.1017/9781009371964

© Amy Gais 2024

This publication is in copyright. Subject to statutory exception and to the provisions of relevant collective licensing agreements, no reproduction of any part may take place without the written permission of Cambridge University Press & Assessment.

First published 2024

A catalogue record for this publication is available from the British Library

Library of Congress Cataloging-in-Publication Data
Names: Gais, Amy, 1987– author.
Title: The coerced conscience / Amy Gais.
Description: Cambridge, United Kingdom ; New York : Cambridge University Press, 2024. | Includes bibliographical references and index.
Identifiers: LCCN 2023027781 | ISBN 9781009372008 (hardback) | ISBN 9781009371964 (ebook)
Subjects: LCSH: Liberty of conscience – Philosophy.
Classification: LCC BV741 .G35 2024 | DDC 261.7/2–dc23/eng/20230828
LC record available at https://lccn.loc.gov/2023027781

ISBN 978-1-009-37200-8 Hardback

Cambridge University Press & Assessment has no responsibility for the persistence or accuracy of URLs for external or third-party internet websites referred to in this publication and does not guarantee that any content on such websites is, or will remain, accurate or appropriate.

For my father

If everybody always lies to you, the consequence is not that you believe the lies, but rather that nobody believes anything any longer.

Hannah Arendt*

* Attibuted to Hannah Arendt, from an interview between Roger Errera and Hannah Arendt. Copyright © 1978 by Hannah Arendt. First appeared in the October 26 1978 edition of the *New York Review of Books*. Reprinted by permission of Georges Borchardt, Inc., on behalf of the Hannah Arendt Bluecher Literary Trust.

Contents

Acknowledgments		*page* viii
A Note on Texts and Abbreviations		xiii
1	A New Kind of Politics	1
2	John Milton and Expressive Conscience	22
3	Thomas Hobbes and Instilled Conscience	41
4	Baruch Spinoza and Conscientious Speech	69
5	Pierre Bayle and Tormented Conscience	91
6	The Politics of Conscience	108
	Bibliography	137
	Index	148

Acknowledgments

This book could not have been written without the love and support of my friends, family, and colleagues. It is a privilege to acknowledge them here.

This book began as a dissertation during my Ph.D. at Yale University, and I remain grateful to my dissertation committee, Bryan Garsten, Steven Smith, and Ian Shapiro, for their intellectual generosity and steadfast encouragement. My greatest debt is to my mentor and dissertation chair, Bryan, whose encouragement throughout my academic career has been unwavering. He read every iteration of this project generously, yet critically, and offered the next right piece of advice to help me move forward. During the difficult (and I now know, inevitable) part of the process when I could not yet see the whole of the project, he gently encouraged me to keep going. I will always be grateful to him for that kindness. Steven's generosity of spirit and ferocious intellect helped shape this project, and even more broadly, enriched my time at Yale. Ian's support throughout the Ph.D. was resolute. His confidence that I would be a great scholar and teacher meant more to me than I can express here. As an external reader, Karuna Mantena urged me to consider whether the motivating question of the project hinged on my curiosity about religion and politics or, more broadly, about oppression, an illuminating question that shaped the final version of this manuscript and continues to inform my research.

I also benefited immensely from the companionship of and conversations with many friends and colleagues at Yale, including Stephanie Almeida, Consuelo Amat, Alyssa Battistoni, Teresa Bejan, Stefan Eich, Adom Getachew, Lisa Gilson, Aaron Greenberg, Mie Inouye, Anna Jurkevics, Max Krahé, Lizzie Krontiris, Hélène Landemore, Paul Linden-Retek, Karuna Mantena, Luke Mayville,

ACKNOWLEDGMENTS   ix

Guilia Oskian, Travis Pantin, Erin Pineda, Hari Ramesh, Andrew Sabl, Nica Siegel, Anurag Sinha, and Alicia Steinmetz. In particular, Anna modeled ambition, leadership, and grace for me during our time at Yale. I am especially grateful to her for founding the Women's Political Theory Writing Group, a community that cultivated my voice during graduate school and deepened my understanding of ways to make the university a more just and equitable place to learn and work. My work at Yale was generously supported by the Yale University Teaching and Dissertation Fellowships, the US Department of Education, and the Beinecke Rare Book & Manuscript Library.

Before Yale, I had the great fortune of studying political theory at the University of Chicago and Tufts University. I continue to enjoy the friendship of my mentor at Chicago, John McCormick. There are very few people whose generosity rivals their intellect, and John is one of these rare individuals. I owe him a special debt for helping me find my way to Yale. At Chicago, Julie Cooper brought Hobbes to life for me and inspired me to explore early modern political thought. Together, John and Julie, as well as Patchen Markell and Sankar Muthu, taught me about the kinds of questions that might be worth asking and how I might try to answer them. My friends and comrades at Chicago, including Jessica Cooper, Sofia Fenner, Steven Klein, Daniel Nichanian, Ethan Porter, and Ali Sutherland-Brown, were a wonderful introduction to what it means to be a part of an intellectual community. At Tufts, Vickie Sullivan and Robert Devigne introduced me to the discipline of political theory and cultivated my unabashed love of ideas. Janis Freedman-Bellow fostered my intellectual curiosity and urged me to see the political in the personal. There could have been no better preparation for my Ph.D. than my time at Chicago and Tufts.

I finished this book at Washington University in St. Louis, with financial support from the Andrew W. Mellon Foundation, where my colleagues welcomed me into the intellectual community and continue to engage generously with my work. I owe an incalculable debt to my mentor and colleague, Joseph Loewenstein, who has enriched my time at WashU with his intellectual precision, professional guidance, and much-appreciated wit. He has facilitated so much of my intellectual and professional development at WashU. I have also benefited immensely from the intellectual support and engagement of many friends and colleagues at WashU, including Jami Ake, Matthew Babb, Anna Bialek, David Cunningham, Meg Galindo, Marie Griffith, Clarissa Hayward, John Inazu, Matthew Kelley, Clare Kim, Allison Korinek, Frank Lovett, Lerone Martin, Paige McGinley, Philip Purchase, Matthew Rickard, Leigh Schmidt, Mark Valeri, Abram Van Engen, Anna Whittington, and Steven Zwicker. I am a much stronger scholar, teacher, and thinker than when I first arrived in St. Louis, a testament to their intellectual generosity and commitment to interdisciplinary inquiry. Lastly, I was humbled by the great care and constructive spirit with which Alison McQueen, Lucas Swaine, Frank Lovett, Steven Zwicker, and Joe Loewenstein, participated in my book manuscript conference at WashU. The scope and depth of the participants' comments were truly impressive, and their insights and questions pushed me to strengthen the book's overall argument and refine my interventions. This book is a much stronger one because of their thoughtful and constructive feedback.

I have also benefited immensely from the research assistance of Maya Horn and Julia Cleary. Over the last three years, Maya grew to be more of an intellectual interlocutor than an undergraduate research assistant. I owe a great intellectual debt to her for sharpening my own thinking, and I look forward to seeing where her immense talent takes her in life. Julia inherited this project in its concluding stage and has been invaluable in helping me polish the final version of the manuscript. I presented many iterations of this project to diverse intellectual audiences on campus, including the Workshop on Politics, Ethics, and Society, the John C. Danforth Center on Religion and Politics Colloquium, and the Early Modern Reading Group. I am grateful to the many participants of these workshops for their constructive and charitable feedback.

ACKNOWLEDGMENTS xi

I value being a part of a broader intellectual community of political theorists, including Yuna Blajer de la Garza, Stefan Eich, Lisa Gilson, Jennie Ikuta, Desmond Jagmohan, Glory Liu, Alison McQueen, Erin Pineda, Melvin Rogers, and Alicia Steinmetz. In particular, I am grateful for the intellectual and professional friendship and support of Glory, Yuna, and Alicia, with whom I have developed a new Women's Writing Group, modeled on Anna's back at Yale. These three brilliant women enrich my research, teaching, and life in academia.

It has been a dream come true to publish my first book with Cambridge University Press. I am grateful to the editorial and production team at Cambridge who shepherded this book through the publication process, including my editor, Robert Dreesen, as well as Erika Walsh, Sable Gravesandy, Claire Sissen, and Santhamurthy Ramamoorthy. Robert enthusiastically embraced this project from the beginning and secured excellent external reviewers, a logistical triumph during the COVID-19 pandemic. I am immensely grateful to the two anonymous external reviewers who helped me sharpen the focus of this book in the final revision stage. Erika, Sable, Claire, and Santha provided attentive editorial support at each stage of the publication process. Earlier versions of parts of Chapter 3, 4, and 5 appeared, respectively, as "Thomas Hobbes and 'Gently Instilled' Conscience" in *History of European Ideas* 47, no. 8 (2021), 1211–1227, and "The Politics of Hypocrisy: Baruch Spinoza and Pierre Bayle on Hypocritical Conformity," in *Political Theory* 48, no. 5 (2020), 588–614. I am grateful to these journals for allowing me to reproduce the relevant portions of those texts here.

I am grateful to my friends for their support and encouragement during this process, including Consuelo Amat, Sofia Fenner, Adrienne Frieden, Jocelyn Gordon, Samantha Kindler, Carolyn Stoner, Ali Sutherland-Brown, and Kelley Vendeland. To Carolyn, I promise to not lose sight of shared driveways (or perhaps, even more importantly, shared offices). Sofia has been one step ahead of me in this strange career and graciously passed along her hard-earned insight at each stage. Her fierce devotion and beautiful spirit are lovely by-products of our shared vocation. Jocelyn embodies female friendship by celebrating my many successes and reframing my many setbacks. It is a daily joy to support her and be supported by her.

The love and support of my family during this endeavor has been steadfast and their home a welcomed respite from the vicissitudes of an academic career. It is a tremendous joy to dedicate this book to my father, Marc Rabinowitz, without whom I would not have been able to write this book. I will never be able to repay his commitment to me and our family, but I hope that this dedication shows him that it has not gone unrecognized.

My greatest debt is to my husband, Jonathon Gais, for his love and partnership. I am proud of this book, but the thing that I am proudest of is being loved by him, Thomas, and Jacqueline.

A Note on Texts and Abbreviations

Texts by John Milton, Thomas Hobbes, Baruch Spinoza, and Pierre Bayle are cited frequently in this book. The following abbreviations will be used in parenthetical citations.

MILTON

CPW   *Complete Prose Works of John Milton, Volume 1–8*, ed. Don Wolfe (New Haven, CT: Yale University Press, 1953–1982).

HOBBES

DC   *De Cive*, ed. Richard Tuck and Michael Silverthorne (New York: Cambridge University Press, 1998).

L   *Thomas Hobbes: Leviathan, Volume 1–3*, ed. Noel Malcolm (Oxford: Clarendon Press, 2012).

B   *Behemoth, or Long Parliament*, ed. Ferdinand Tönnies (Chicago: University of Chicago Press, 1990).

SPINOZA

TPT   *The Collected Works of Spinoza, Volume 1–2*, ed. and trans. Edwin Curley (Princeton: Princeton University Press, 2016).

BAYLE

PC   *A Philosophical Commentary on These Words of the Gospel, Luke 14.23, "Compel Them to Come In, That My House May be Full,"* ed. John Kilcullen and Chandran Kukathas (Indianapolis: Liberty Fund, 2005).

I A New Kind of Politics

In 1644, John Milton, the English poet and polemicist, made an impassioned plea on behalf of liberty of conscience to Parliament: "Give me the liberty to know, to utter, and to argue freely according to conscience, above all liberties."[1] Nearly three centuries later, Milton's powerful words were chiseled into the marble facade of the Chicago Tribune Tower, a visual symbol of his influence on American democracy and the significance of liberty of conscience to modern notions of freedom. Liberty of conscience – the freedom to follow one's religious beliefs – is often taken for granted today.[2] Individuals should be free, we assume, to live their lives in accordance with the dictates of conscience, without encroachment from religious or political authorities, and individuals may be exempt from obligations to the state when their innermost conviction conflicts with democratic laws and norms. This fundamental freedom has long enjoyed esteem, enshrined in the First Amendment of the US Constitution and revered throughout Western history. The influential political philosopher John Rawls recognizes the profound importance of liberty of conscience in any just and free society, characterizing it as a "basic liberty" with an "essential place in any constitutional democracy."[3] Cécile Laborde affirms this received view, stressing that liberty of conscience is the "most conclusively

---

[1] John Milton, *Complete Prose Works of John Milton, Volume 2*, ed. Don Wolfe (New Haven, CT: Yale University Press, 1953–1982), 560. Hereafter cited in parenthetical citations as CPW with volume and page number.

[2] The Oxford English Dictionary defines the "freedom of conscience" as the "right to follow one's own beliefs in matters of religion and morality." *Oxford English Dictionary*, s.v. "freedom of conscience," accessed September 20, 2017, https://en.oxforddictionaries.com/definition/freedom_of_conscience.

[3] John Rawls, *Political Liberalism: Expanded Edition* (New York: Columbia University Press, 2005), 312, 461.

I

2 A NEW KIND OF POLITICS

justified, and least controversial liberal freedom," among a broader constellation of freedoms.[4] While Milton's impassioned plea on behalf of liberty of conscience, the liberty "above all [other] liberties," was quite radical in his time, liberty of conscience has become largely "settled" today.[5]

This widespread consensus is hardly unwarranted. Influential figures throughout Western history are celebrated for their profound courage and resolute unwillingness to compromise their conscience when confronted with oppressive religious and political authorities. Martin Luther invoked liberty of conscience to eschew the mediation of canonical tradition and ecclesiastical authority in the Protestant Reformation.[6] Prominent leaders of progressive social movements, such as Henry David Thoreau and Martin Luther King, Jr., appealed to conscience to defend racial equality, civil disobedience, and social justice.[7] Conscientious objection to military conscription has been afforded to American citizens, ranging from protections for Quakers and Mennonites during the American Revolution to conscientious objectors during the Vietnam War.[8] In an early campaign speech, then presidential hopeful Barack Obama advocated for immigration reform, the closing of Guantanamo Bay, and minimum wage legislation by encouraging American citizens to embrace a "new" kind

---

[4] Cécile Laborde, *Liberalism's Religion* (Cambridge, MA: Harvard University Press, 2017), 61.

[5] John Rawls, *A Theory of Justice* (Cambridge, MA: Harvard University Press, 1971), 206.

[6] Abraham Stoll, *Conscience in Early Modern English Literature, Volume 1* (Cambridge: Cambridge University Press, 2017), 13.

[7] Henry David Thoreau, "Resistance to Civil Government," in *Thoreau: Political Writings*, ed. Nancy Rosenblum (Cambridge: Cambridge University Press, 1996); Thoreau, "Conscience Is Instinct Bred in the House," in *Thoreau: Collected Essays and Poems*, ed. Elizabeth Hall Witherell (New York: Penguin, 2001); Martin Luther King Jr., "Letter from a Birmingham City Jail," "Remaining Awake through a Great Revolution, Sermon Delivered on Passion Sunday, March 31, 1968," and "The Trumpet of Conscience," in *A Testament of Hope: The Essential Writings and Speeches of Martin Luther King Jr.*, ed. James Washington (New York: Harper Collins, 1990).

[8] Michael Walzer, *Obligations: Essays on Disobedience, War, and Citizenship* (Cambridge, MA: Harvard University Press, 1970), 120–146.

of politics, "a politics of conscience."[9] Liberty of conscience, Lucas Swaine suggests, is an "important touchstone" in the broader pursuit of religious toleration and political justice in American history.[10]

Yet this venerated freedom is increasingly in dispute. In recent decades, Christian evangelicals have invoked liberty of conscience to justify exemptions from anti-discrimination laws that protect equality among citizens and safeguard L.G.B.T.Q.I.A.+ rights. Kim Davis, a Kentucky county clerk, gained national notoriety for refusing to issue a marriage license after the Supreme Court's landmark ruling to legalize same-sex marriage. In the public statement following her arrest, Davis cast her denial to issue the license in the language of conscience, insisting that "issu[ing] a marriage license which conflicts with God's definition of marriage, with my name affixed to the certificate, would violate my conscience."[11] Jack Phillips, a baker in Colorado, refused to create a wedding cake for a same-sex couple, David Mullins and Charlie Craig, culminating in *Masterpiece Cakeshop* v. *Colorado Civil Rights Commission*.[12] Phillips has become a symbol of the politics of conscience, revealing of the recent politicization and polarization of this longstanding freedom.[13] Phillips is hardly an outlier even if he has dominated public discourse. Only three years after *Masterpiece Cakeshop*, the Supreme Court considered whether the city of Philadelphia could ban the Catholic Social Services for refusing to place foster children with same-sex couples. In the wake of *Obergefell* and a rapidly shifting political and social

---

[9] Barack Obama, "Remarks in Hartford, Connecticut: 'A Politics of Conscience'," *The American Presidency Project*, June 23, 2007, www.presidency.ucsb.edu/ws/?pid=76986.

[10] Lucas Swaine, *Liberal Conscience: Politics and Principle in a World of Religious Pluralism* (New York: Columbia University Press, 2006), 46.

[11] Alan Blinder and Richard Pérez-Peña, "Kentucky Clerk Denies Same-Sex Marriage Licenses, Defying Court," *New York Times*, September 1, 2015, www.nytimes.com/2015/09/02/us/same-sex-marriage-kentucky-kim-davis.html.

[12] Adam Liptak, "In Narrow Decision, Supreme Court Sides with Baker Who Turned Away Gay Couple," *New York Times*, June 4, 2018, www.nytimes.com/2018/06/04/us/politics/supreme-court-sides-with-baker-who-turned-away-gay-couple.html.

[13] Charles McCrary, *Sincerely Held: American Religion, Secularism, and Belief* (Chicago: University of Chicago Press, 2022).

landscape on marriage equality and L.G.B.T.Q.I.A.+ rights, controversies on florists, bakers, and wedding planners who violate anti-discrimination laws are increasingly commonplace.

While *Masterpiece Cakeshop* figures prominently in American public discourse, there are many other cases and controversies on the implications and limits of liberty of conscience.[14] Under the Trump Administration, the Department of Health and Human Services established the Conscience and Religious Freedom Division, tasked with protecting the "conscience rights" of doctors, nurses, and other health-care professionals who refuse to perform abortions or gender reassignment surgery.[15] Liberty of conscience is increasingly contentious in debates on reproductive freedom and abortion access, especially following the erosion of reproductive rights with *Dobbs* v. *Jackson Women's Health Organization*. In *Kennedy* v. *Bremerton*, the Supreme Court upheld a Washington state high-school coach's right to pray with his students immediately after football games. The "culture wars" in American politics seem to have morphed into the "conscience wars," bringing this seemingly innocuous freedom under renewed scrutiny.[16]

Influential commentators, such as Douglas NeJaime and Reva Siegel, suggest that these recent invocations of conscience exceed traditional claims of liberty of conscience to defend the more invasive assertion of an individual's conscientious scruples to the conduct of others.[17] Liberty of conscience, as it is invoked today, is far from the

---

[14] On the difference between Kim Davis and Jack Phillips, especially in terms of whiteness and masculinity, see McCrary, *Sincerely Held*, 238, 242–243, 246–247, 252, 257–260, 262–264.

[15] Robert Pear and Jeremy W. Peters, "Trump Gives Health Workers New Religious Liberty Protections," *New York Times*, January 18, 2018, www.nytimes.com/2018/01/18/us/health-care-office-abortion-contraception.html.

[16] Douglas NeJaime and Reva B. Siegel, "Conscience Wars: Complicity-Based Conscience Claims in Religion and Politics," *Yale Law Journal* 124 (2015): 2516–2591; Susanna Mancini and Michel Rosenfeld, eds., *The Conscience Wars: Rethinking the Balance between Religion, Identity, and Equality* (Cambridge: Cambridge University Press, 2018).

[17] NeJaime and Siegel, "Conscience Wars," 2516–2591.

conventional freedom, long respected and upheld in American politics. These recent invocations of liberty of conscience, commentators lament, do not reflect Milton's plea for liberty of conscience chiseled into the Chicago Tribune Tower, but are misappropriations of this freedom. NeJaime and Siegel urge commentators to consider protecting liberty of conscience in a way that advances pluralism and limits the accommodation of complicity-based conscience claims. But if contemporary invocations continue to outreach the established implications of the venerated freedom, perhaps liberty of conscience should be abandoned altogether.

This sustained attention to liberty of conscience in American politics also features in scholarly debates on religion and politics, ranging from secularism, toleration, free speech, blasphemy, to religious extremism. Influential critical theorists, such as Talal Asad, Saba Mahmood, Wendy Brown, and Rainer Forst, criticize liberty of conscience for implicitly favoring Christianity over other religions, such as Islam and Judaism, by prioritizing the inviolable sphere of inward conviction over collective forms of religious life.[18] Liberty of conscience "enshrine[s] a particular conception of religiosity that is deemed normative and worthy of legal protection," safeguarding religions that prioritize religious belief.[19] Liberty of conscience privileges religious conviction by conflating conscience with belief, thereby restricting the state from attempts to invade the inward sphere of the individual or coerce religious belief. The anthropologist of secularism, Talal Asad, stresses the emphasis on "private belief"

---

[18] Talal Asad, *Formations of the Secular: Christianity, Islam, Modernity* (Palo Alto: Stanford University Press, 2003); Saba Mahmood, *Politics of Piety: The Islamic Revival and the Feminist Subject* (Princeton: Princeton University Press, 2011); Wendy Brown, *Regulating Aversion: Tolerance in the Age of Identity and Empire* (Princeton: Princeton University Press, 2008); Talal Asad, Wendy Brown, Judith Butler, and Saba Mahmood, *Is Critique Secular? Blasphemy, Injury, and Free Speech* (New York: Fordham University Press, 2013); Rainer Forst, *Toleration in Conflict: Past and Present* (Cambridge: Cambridge University Press, 2013); Winnifred Sullivan, Elizabeth Shakman Hurd, Saba Mahmood, and Peter Danchin, eds., *Politics of Religious Freedom* (Chicago: University of Chicago Press, 2015).

[19] Asad, *Formations of the Secular*, 50.

above other expressions or manifestations of religion.[20] Building on Asad, Saba Mahmood laments the conflation of "belief, conscience, and individual choice" in the modern understanding of religion.[21] By prioritizing the inviolable sphere of inward conviction over collective forms of religious life, such as daily prayer, communal worship, or religious dress, liberty of conscience implicitly legitimizes Christianity, and more specifically, Protestantism, and fails to protect religious practices which are central to Islam and Judaism.

For these critics, liberty of conscience does not endow religious dissenters with *too* much authority to refute democratic laws and norms but disciplines citizens into individualistic, liberal subjects and limits religious practice. Liberty of conscience might, for example, protect an individual's right to believe in the importance of modesty, but it does not safeguard the right of a Muslim woman to wear a headscarf in certain public spaces, even if veiling is a manifestation of her innermost commitment to modesty or the means through which *taqwa* (piety or closeness to God) is cultivated in the first place. Islamic veiling belongs "to the realm of practices, not to the realm of belief," revealing the deep incompatibility between liberty of conscience and the lived experience of religion as it is practiced by Muslims, Jews, Catholics, Sikhs, and Christians all over the world.[22] Liberty of conscience is ill-equipped to accommodate the deep religious pluralism which characterizes our modern world, urging critical theorists to consider abandoning it altogether.[23]

These influential critiques of liberty of conscience are often attributed to the intellectual origins of the concept. Liberty of conscience privileges a Christian, and more specifically, Protestant, understanding of religiosity because the concept emerged triumphantly in John Milton's world – early modernity. Liberty of

---

[20] Talal Asad, "Thinking about Religion, Belief, and Politics," in *Cambridge Companion to Religious Studies*, ed. Robert Orsi (Cambridge: Cambridge University Press, 2012), 41.

[21] Ibid., 50.

[22] Laborde, *Liberalism's Religion*, 22.

[23] Ibid., 4.

conscience "acquired new urgency and importance" in early modernity as religious dissenters were forced to navigate conflicting commitments between their repressive sovereigns and tender consciences in a newly multiconfessional society.[24] Religious persecution was commonplace in seventeenth-century European society, and religious dissenters navigated living under the hostility of persecutory conditions. Against the "impressive intellectual, ideological, and political edifice" of religious persecution, religious dissenters defended toleration and liberty of conscience in seventeenth-century Europe.[25]

Liberty of conscience, commentators suggest, is a begrudging solution to religious conflicts across Western Europe and the American colonies following the Protestant Reformation. For Rawls, the "historical origin of political liberalism [and] ... the liberty of conscience" can be traced to the "Reformation and its aftermath, with the long controversies over religious toleration" in early modernity.[26] Asad shares this received historical genealogy of liberty of conscience, stressing that the concept "rests on a new religious psychology and a new concept of the state that were beginning to emerge in seventeenth-century Europe."[27] For both influential advocates and critics of liberty of conscience, the concept bears the heavy imprint of its intellectual origins. In light of its early modern intellectual roots and its corresponding deficiencies, some political theorists, such as Charles Taylor and Cécile Laborde, have sought to reconceive of liberty of conscience as a more inclusive freedom,[28] while other critical theorists, such as Saba Mahmood and Rainer Forst, have recommended abandoning it altogether.[29] But is this received

---

[24] Perez Zagorin, *Ways of Lying: Dissimulation, Persecution and Conformity in Early Modern Europe* (Cambridge, MA: Harvard University Press, 1990), 68.

[25] Andrew Murphy, *Liberty, Conscience, and Toleration: The Political Thought of William Penn* (Oxford: Oxford University Press, 2015), 36.

[26] Rawls, *Political Liberalism*, xxiv.

[27] Asad, "Thinking about Religion, Belief, and Politics," 43.

[28] Jocelyn Maclure and Charles Taylor, *Secularism and Freedom of Conscience* (Cambridge, MA: Harvard University Press, 2011); Laborde, *Liberalism's Religion*, 19–20.

[29] Rainer Forst, *Toleration in Conflict: Past and Present* (Cambridge: Cambridge University Press, 2013); Saba Mahmood, *Religious Difference in a Secular Age: A Minority Report* (Princeton: Princeton University Press, 2015).

historical account of liberty of conscience an accurate representation of the freedom of liberty of conscience as it emerged in early modernity? And to what extent should we continue to uphold it today, especially given its encroachment on democracy and equality?

This book argues that liberty of conscience remains a crucial freedom worth protecting because safeguarding it prevents political, social, and psychological threats to freedom. Influential early modern theorists of toleration, John Milton, Thomas Hobbes, Baruch Spinoza, and Pierre Bayle, I show, defend liberty of conscience by stressing the unanticipated repercussions of conformity. By recovering the intellectual origins of liberty of conscience in early modern politics and situating influential theorists of toleration in overlooked historical debates on religious dissimulation and hypocritical conformity, I demonstrate that infringements on conscience risk impeding political engagement, eroding civic trust, and inciting religious fanaticism. While this is a book about freedom, it is also arguably a book about *threats* to freedom, specifically conformity, hypocrisy, and persecution. It considers the social, psychological, and political harms done by political refusals to tolerate religious differences and allow individuals to practice their religion freely in accordance with the dictates of conscience. By returning to a historical context in which liberty of conscience was not granted to religious dissenters – but rather, actively denied – this book foregrounds Bayle's argument that coercing conscience exacerbates religious fervor and inflicts significant psychological harm on dissenters, thereby undermining the goal of cultivating social cohesion in politics. In controversies on the politics of conscience, I suggest that we acknowledge that refusals to tolerate claims of conscience – while perhaps well-grounded on democratic laws and norms – might exacerbate conscientious fervor and empower resentment against the state. This Baylean intuition does not necessarily tell us where to draw the limits of toleration – what should be tolerated and what goes beyond the pale – but it does tell us something about how to approach invocations of conscience and what to expect when we deem something intolerable.

By returning to the intellectual origins of liberty of conscience, I resist a historical claim often made by its critics – that this freedom is newly contentious or that recent invocations of liberty of conscience misappropriate the freedom in unprecedented ways. Liberty of conscience is vulnerable today, and perhaps fairly so given its recent invocations against equality and dignity, but this book engages in the crucial work of recovering the history and meaning of liberty of conscience to show that even influential theorists of liberty of conscience acknowledge its contentiousness. While these figures all concede its intractability, they differ in their approach to this problem. Hobbes attempts to correct for this intractability with civic education, and Milton, Spinoza, and Bayle theorize distinct strategies to manage its threat to political stability. Beyond demonstrating that liberty of conscience has been polarizing throughout its history, this book suggests that early modern figures offer us intuitions into how to manage the polarizing politics of liberty of conscience and how best to approach placing limits on liberty of conscience.

These four influential early modern figures deserve our attention for two reasons, one historical and the other conceptual. First, they are active participants in political debates on toleration and liberty of conscience, often at great risk to their security and status. For these figures, these debates were not an abstract intellectual exercise, but a deeply fraught crisis that immediately impacted their own lives, their families, and their political communities. Indeed, all four of these figures were marginalized, ostracized, and even persecuted for their heterodox political and religious views during their own lifetimes. Their volatile context brings a profound urgency to their writing that makes them feel relevant even today, especially as liberty of conscience reemerges as a contentious concept. Second, they – like us – struggle with the precarious balancing act between conscience and law. On one hand, they defend the liberation of conscience from the coercive reach of the state, but on the other, they recognize that unlicensed liberty of conscience amounts to political chaos; on one hand, they acknowledge that there are meaningful costs to infringements on conscience, but on the other, they are not sanguine enough to assume liberty of conscience should be absolute. By offering distinct answers to this difficult balancing act, these four figures remind us that this difficulty is hardly unprecedented.

By situating influential theorists of liberty of conscience in early modern debates on hypocritical conformity and religious dissimulation, this book showcases overlooked justifications for toleration in early modern political thought, specifically psychological defenses of toleration. Over the course of the book, I draw out their engagement with hypocritical conformity in their broader theories of toleration and liberty of conscience, recovering what I call Milton's *expressive conscience*, Hobbes's *instilled conscience*, Spinoza's *conscientious speech*, and Bayle's *tormented conscience*. This sustained attention to their views of hypocritical conformity, I suggest, demonstrates that these figures were shaped considerably by their concerns with conformity and hypocrisy, specifically the deleterious effects of disengagement, distrust, and distress propagated by the "pervasive and even overwhelming reality" of religious persecution across early modern Europe.[30] Revisionist accounts have qualified the "heroic tale of progress" often associated with early modernity, showing that early modern Europe was hardly characterized by "progressive" institutional arrangements and shared attitudes toward religious dissenters.[31] While Queen Elizabeth I famously refused to "make windows into men's souls," confessional conflicts, religious persecution, and outward conformity remained commonplace features of

[30] Zagorin, *Ways of Lying*, 255.

[31] Jeffrey Collins, "Redeeming the Enlightenment: New Histories of Religious Toleration," *The Journal of Modern History* 81, no. 3 (2009), 609; Alexandra Walsham, "Ordeals of Conscience: Casuistry, Conformity, and Confessional Identity in Post-Reformation England," in *Contexts of Conscience in Early Modern Europe, 1500–1700*, ed. Harald Braun and Edward Vallance (New York: Palgrave Macmillan, 2004), 32–48; Alexandra Walsham, *Charitable Hatred: Tolerance and Intolerance in England, 1500–1700* (Manchester: Manchester University Press, 2006), especially 1–13, 39–92, 160–162, 188–206; Benjamin Kaplan, *Divided by Faith: Religious Conflict and the Practice of Toleration in Early Modern Europe* (Cambridge, MA: Harvard University Press, 2007), especially 1–47, 127–133, 140–143, 156–171, 177–183, 195–197.

early modern political and social life.[32] In a newly multiconfessional society, religious dissenters were forced to choose among "martyrdom, insurrection and emigration to dissimulation, equivocation and forms of partial and occasional conformity," to survive persecutory conditions.[33] Many religious dissenters were not afforded liberty of conscience in early modernity but conformed to the state religion to avoid financial penalties, imprisonment, or violent death.[34] The inevitable consequence of this widespread religious persecution was not an erasure of the fact of religious pluralism, but the ubiquity of hypocritical conformity and religious dissimulation. This hypocritical conformity ranged from disingenuous participation in mandatory religious services to the equivocation of certain religious proclamations, such as refusing to bow one's head or using a muddled voice during a prayer. Many acquiesced to the state religion publicly while continuing to practice their religion privately in hidden worship spaces (i.e., conventicles) or family homes (i.e., house chapels).[35] While some degree of equivocation is arguably characteristic of all

---

[32] Zagorin, *Ways of Lying*, 68; Benjamin Kaplan, *Divided by Faith*, 115, 157–158, 161; Andrew Hadfield, *Lying in Early Modern English Culture: From the Oath of Supremacy to the Oath of Allegiance* (Oxford: Oxford University Press, 2017), 1–20; Alexandra Walsham, "Ordeals of Conscience," 36–37; Alexandra Walsham, *Charitable Hatred*, 188–206.

[33] Walsham, *Charitable Hatred*, 161.

[34] I use gender-neutral language to refer to religious dissenters, yet this decision is not historically accurate. Most religious dissenters that engaged in hypocritical conformity were men, since women (and their children) were often excluded from the public sphere and public displays of religious obedience. Alexandra Walsham documents the gendered practice of hypocritical conformity: "a shrewd domestic arrangement prevailed, whereby the husband periodically conformed to protect the family's social respectability and financial security, while his wife and children safeguarded its spiritual integrity by strictly separation themselves from heretical worship" (Walsham, *Charitable Hatred*, 191). Benjamin Kaplan also recognizes the gender dynamics of hypocritical conformity, suggesting that more men were forced to conform than women and children. Yet he acknowledges that the state was less concerned with the conformity of women and children, as the conformity of men was a sufficient "gesture of submission authorities required to leave their families alone" (Kaplan, *Divided by Faith*, 275). I also use male pronouns in the substantive chapters on early modern political thought to refer to the political subject since many of these figures exclude women from the purview of politics.

[35] Kaplan, *Divided by Faith*, 172–197.

social interactions, the severity and ubiquity of religious persecution in early modern Europe was so drastic that it actively "encouraged [dissenters] to hide behind a façade of outward conformity."[36] Intellectual debates on hypocritical conformity and religious dissimulation were central to early modern debates on toleration and liberty of conscience: to what extent should the state compel attendance at liturgical services and sacramental rights or the public profession of obedience and allegiance, even when this conformity violates the conscience of dissenters?

Then, like now, the question of what liberty of conscience entails was contested. For both early modern theorists of toleration and contemporary advocates of liberty of conscience, the freedom is often viewed as implying the liberation of inward conviction. Some early modern figures argue that "the restriction of certain practices" is "compatible" with liberty of conscience, suggesting that an individual cannot "publish his opinions, and entangle the consciences of others."[37] Others argue that liberty of conscience extends beyond an "internal judge of individual action," to protect a "wide range of action in accordance with conscience."[38] Early modern debates on liberty of conscience center on the "exercis[ing] of religious conscience" in cases when the laws and norms of the state conflict with the conscience of the individual.[39] By showcasing the deep contestation over the meaning and implications of liberty of conscience in early modern political thought, this book challenges the prevailing assumption that liberty of conscience is a static, monolithic concept with early modern underpinnings; rather, I show that even influential early modern figures offer competing – even contradictory – understandings of liberty of conscience. The episodic account of these four figures dramatizes this contestation by recovering the

[36] Walsham, *Charitable Hatred*, 206.

[37] Andrew Murphy, *Conscience and Community: Revisiting Toleration and Religious Dissent in Early Modern England and America* (University Park, PN: Pennsylvania State University Press, 2001), 118.

[38] Murphy, *Liberty, Conscience, and Toleration*, 43.

[39] Ibid., 200.

A NEW KIND OF POLITICS 13

plurality of the concept in early modern political thought and demonstrating that the concept has a far more controversial history and meaning than commentators often acknowledge today. The politicization and polarization of liberty of conscience are urgent today and reflect the peculiarities of our specific historical context, but they are hardly new.

By engaging with this cast of early modern figures, this book decenters one figure who dominates historical narratives on toleration: John Locke. In standard narratives on the "rise of religious toleration," Locke is often cast as the hero in the "liberal" triumph of toleration over "backward" religious persecution,[40] inspiring what John Dunn has flippantly called the "Locke obsession."[41] Locke acknowledges the futility of coercion to inspire genuine conversion, suggesting that persecution merely pressures dissenters into insincere acquiescence. Recent work on Locke, however, challenges this received portrait of Locke as a minimal defender of toleration by showing that even "Locke [does not] seem particularly 'Lockean.'"[42] Many commentators stress that Locke is more complicated than received accounts suggest, either offering far more than a minimal defense of toleration or changing his view of the limits of toleration over the course of his writings. This book complements these revisionist

[40] Kaplan, *Divided by Faith*, 6.
[41] John Dunn, *The Political Thought of John Locke* (Cambridge: Cambridge University Press, 1969), xi.
[42] Teresa Bejan, *Mere Civility: Toleration and Its Limits in Early Modern England and America* (Cambridge, MA: Harvard University Press, 2017), 138. For revisionist accounts of Locke, see Jeremy Waldron, "Locke, Toleration and the Rationality of Persecution" in *Justifying Toleration: Conceptual and Historical Approaches*, ed. Susan Mendus (Cambridge: Cambridge University Press, 1988), 61–86; Kirstie McClure, "Differences, Diversity, and the Limits of Toleration," *Political Theory* 18 (1990), 361–391; Ingrid Creppell, "Locke on Toleration: The Transformation of Constraint," *Political Theory* 24 (1996), 200–240; Alex Tuckness, "Rethinking the Intolerant Locke," *American Journal of Political Science* 46, no. 2 (2002), 288–298; Jeremy Waldron, *God, Locke, and Equality* (Cambridge: Cambridge University Press, 2002), 217–243; John Marshall, *John Locke, Toleration, and Early Enlightenment Culture* (Cambridge: Cambridge University Press, 2006); Forst, *Toleration in Conflict*, 170–265; Duncan Bell, "What Is Liberalism?" *Political Theory* 42, no. 6 (2014): 682–715; Bejan, *Mere Civility*, 113–143; Jeffrey Collins, *In the Shadow of Leviathan: John Locke and the Politics of Conscience* (Cambridge: Cambridge University Press, 2020).

14 A NEW KIND OF POLITICS

efforts by engaging in a shared endeavor to complicate received views of other early modern theorists of toleration. By attending to Locke's contemporaries and deepening our understanding of their justifications for liberty of conscience, this book enriches our understanding of the history of toleration, more broadly, in the discipline of political theory.

The sustained attention to hypocritical conformity and religious dissimulation in this book complements scholarly accounts in political theory which emphasize the futility of coercion in early modern defenses of toleration and liberty of conscience. Recent excellent work in early modern political thought by Julie Cooper, Andrew Murphy, Teresa Bejan, and Alison McQueen attends to the political and theological context against which early modern figures were writing to complicate received views of canonical early modern figures.[43] While these commentators deepen our understanding of the nuances in early modern political thought, they overwhelmingly frame early modern defenses of toleration as grounded in a recognition of the futility of coercion to inspire genuine conversion. As Murphy has noted, "a key component of the tolerationist program had always been the idea that 'belief cannot be forced': that, at most, force could produce hypocrites, but never authentic conversion."[44] This scholarly consensus is surely justified. Influential early modern

---

[43] Julie Cooper, *Secular Powers: Humility in Modern Political Thought* (Chicago: University of Chicago Press, 2013); Andrew Murphy, *Liberty, Conscience, and Toleration: The Political Thought of William Penn* (Oxford: Oxford University Press, 2015); Teresa Bejan, *Mere Civility: Toleration and Its Limits in Early Modern England and America* (Cambridge, MA: Harvard University Press, 2017); Alison McQueen, *Political Realism in Apocalyptic Times* (Cambridge: Cambridge University Press, 2018).

[44] Murphy, *Liberty, Conscience, and Toleration*, 249. Asad also stresses this point and attributes it to Locke, although many early modern views of toleration and persecution hinged on this assumption: "Perhaps a more common view is that belief cannot – in the sense of impossibility – be coerced. That is the core of Locke's theory of toleration and one part of the genealogy of secularism.... These shifts in epistemology and politics allowed Locke to insist that the prince's attempt to coerce religious belief – including belief in the implications of religious practices for salvation – was irrational because it could not be done" (Asad, "Thinking about Religion, Belief, and Politics," 43).

proponents of toleration – even many of the figures featured in this book – argue that persecution fails to inspire genuine conversion.

This recognition of the futility of coercion, moreover, aligns with revisionist efforts by political theorists to highlight the "pragmatic" quality of toleration, not grounded in a "positive virtue" but rather in a "grudging acceptance of unpleasant realities."[45] Toleration implies an "often grudgingly negotiated social practice," rather than an inclusive recognition or celebration of difference.[46] For many critics, toleration should be put aside for "something more," such as "respect, recognition, [or] even acceptance" to support and sustain our modern, diverse world.[47] Yet this nuanced attention to the futility of persecution and the limits of toleration, more broadly, does not account for the psychological underpinnings of early modern toleration and liberty of conscience. For influential early modern theorists of toleration, liberty of conscience does not merely hinge on the inefficacy of persecution but on the social mistrust bred by hypocritical conformity to the state religion and the mental torture inflicted on dissenters forced to internalize the disingenuous division between their private and public selves. By showcasing early modern critiques of hypocritical conformity and religious dissimulation, I broaden our understanding of the social, political, and psychic dynamics of liberty of conscience.

Milton's *expressive conscience* suggests that liberty of conscience requires the freedom to express one's innermost commitments to others, specifically in speech and writing. Hypocritical conformity, Milton argues, robs individuals of crucial opportunities to foster political capacities of citizenship, specifically the skill of independent judgment. Milton hints at an intuition that other early modern figures will later foreground – that hypocritical conformity to the state religion hardens dissenters and makes them incapable of being judicious political citizens. If individuals live in a political society that does not

[45] Kaplan, *Divided by Faith*, 8.
[46] Laborde, *Liberalism's Religion*, 16.
[47] Teresa Bejan, "Recent Work on Toleration," *Review of Politics*, 80 (2018), 701.

afford them liberty of conscience, they will slowly lose the capability to exercise their conscience over time. This freedom requires a robust view of freedom and agency in the public sphere since it implies far more than an inward freedom of conviction. Conscience must be cultivated independently of political and ecclesiastical authorities and requires confrontation with other individuals in the public sphere, implying the open exchange of ideas and the freedom to express one's ideas publicly in writing or speech. Milton insists that the circulation of ideas in print allows for an extended opportunity for individuals to exercise their conscience, as the written word persists over time longer than speech which dissipates in the immediate moment, only to be recounted by witnesses. Liberty of conscience is so crucial to Milton's understanding of freedom that he describes it as the highest liberty above all liberties, even justifying other political freedoms.

While Milton offers an impassioned plea on behalf of liberty of conscience, Hobbes condemns liberty of conscience by stressing its incendiary repercussions on social stability and political sovereignty. Religious dissenters fashion themselves as sovereigns, Hobbes warns, emboldening them to do whatever they want rather than obey the state. Hobbes's *instilled conscience* views invocations to conscience as mere assertions of opinion – deeply held and felt, such that individuals insist on acting in accordance with them, but opinions nonetheless. While Hobbes anticipates the danger of liberty of conscience, he also offers a potential solution to this very problem – civic education – and invites us to reflect on how we might cultivate consensus through attempts to shape the conscience of dissenters. The possibility of peaceful coexistence becomes, at some point, about the project of persuasion, for Hobbes, such that invocations of conscience will abate over time and the threat of liberty of conscience to political authority may be tamed.

Spinoza offers a more measured approach to liberty of conscience, an underappreciated compromise between the Miltonic defense of unfettered liberty of conscience and the Hobbesian demand for hypocritical conformity. Like Hobbes, Spinoza recognizes that liberty of conscience conflicts with political sovereignty and social stability. Dissenters are asking, Spinoza acknowledges, to be exempt from their obligations to their political communities and withdraw their compliance and cooperation from the state. Some degree of hypocritical conformity is necessary, Spinoza concedes, for a political society to function. Individuals cannot be free to do whatever they like, even if their conscience conflicts with the law. Yet Spinoza also recognizes that hypocritical conformity has its own pernicious repercussions, specifically the corrosion of civic trust. Spinoza's *conscientious speech* warns that conformity corrodes the social trust that undergirds politics since individuals are not able to confidently assess the sincerity of their citizens. Spinoza aims to reconcile this tension by distinguishing speech from action; dissenters must conform to the law, even if it conflicts with their conscience, but they should be able to express their conscience freely in speech.

While Spinoza emphasizes the social repercussions of hypocritical conformity, Bayle invites us to reflect on the psychological effects of conformity on the dissenter himself, forced to violate his conscience, as well as the counterintuitive implications of this infringement. Bayle's *tormented conscience* suggests that infringements on conscience are experienced as deep violations by the dissenter, arguably just as unsettling as more violent forms of discipline and coercion. The experience of conforming to the state religion does not merely corrode mutual understanding among citizens but asks individuals to endure the taxing experience of suppressing and violating their consciences. Hypocritical conformity is not merely a trivial demand with little consequence for their integrity, as advocates of religious persecution insist, but a deeply felt violation that reverberates even long after the act of conformity is finished. Even more discerningly, Bayle recognizes that hypocritical conformity exacerbates conscientious fervor. Hypocritical conformity does not merely fail to inspire genuine conversion, but it also radicalizes dissenters and urges them to be even more committed to their conscience. In an attempt to transform dissenters through hypocritical conformity, the state risks emboldening dissenters even further and inciting backlash against the state. To the extent that there is a hero in this book, it is Bayle. Even if liberty of conscience cannot be unequivocally tolerated, I argue that we should heed Bayle's warning to treat unaccommodated conscience with respect to abate the unforeseen implications of restrictions on the expression of conscience in the world. Bayle's *tormented conscience* urges us to consider, I argue, why we should respect conscience even if we cannot tolerate it in a pluralistic society.

The conclusion of this book bridges past and present to consider pressing controversies on religious freedom and liberty of conscience in American politics today, specifically two case studies from across the political spectrum. The former concerns a florist who refuses to design floral arrangements for a same-sex wedding, and the latter concerns a humanitarian aid worker who harbors undocumented migrants at the US–Mexico border. These political debates are often presented as balancing acts between the dignity and equality of marginalized individuals, on the one hand, and religious freedom, on the other hand. Of course, these are important concerns worth our careful consideration, but the stakes of these controversies are broader and more contentious than they seem. This is, it is worth acknowledging, not good news. These controversies are already polarizing, dividing families and communities across American society; yet one of the prerequisites for a more tolerant and free society is a deeper understanding of the roadblocks that lie ahead of us.

Milton and his contemporaries resist all-or-nothing approaches to liberty of conscience that often dominate contemporary debates, such as confining liberty of conscience to the inner sphere of the mind or endowing it with absolute authority, a kind of "trump card" that justifies any and all dissent. These two absolutist approaches to liberty of conscience fail to appreciate insights gleaned from early modern debates on hypocritical conformity and religious dissimulation. Milton and Bayle appreciate why infringements on conscience are so deeply felt by dissenters, and Hobbes and Spinoza stress the social and political disorder inherent in invocations of conscience. Over the course of this book, I register the myriad of ways in which each figure sharpens our thinking about liberty of conscience, and in the end, I side with Bayle in his recognition of the psychological infringement of hypocritical conformity worthy of abatement when possible.

While the conclusion invites us to reflect on contemporary controversies on liberty of conscience, it is worth acknowledging that these two historical contexts and the dilemmas of conscience that plague them are hardly the same. I do not mean to equate the two contexts to convince my reader of the immediate relevance of the past to our present. The religious dissenters that are featured in this book were persecuted in ways and to degrees that are deeply foreign to Americans today (although not all religious minorities in the United States and across the world enjoy this freedom). Early modern dissenters did not enjoy the freedom to practice their religion without financial penalties, corporal punishment, imprisonment, or even violence at the hands of the state. Contemporary controversies on liberty of conscience are often concerned with commercial exchanges, for example, rather than mandatory religious services. Religious minorities are arguably not forced to participate in – or forbidden from participating in – religious ceremonies today (again, even this suggestion is more complicated in practice for many religious minorities in America today). The differences between these two contexts are both of degree and kind, and these are crucial to keep in mind as we reflect on the continued relevance of early modern thinkers to the problems of our present.

Yet even contemporary politics seems afflicted by conflicts between conscience and democratic laws and norms that recall the social and psychological fracturing done by early modern practices of religious dissimulation. While American democracy no longer coerces citizens into the kind of hypocritical conformity that was commonplace in early modernity, there are many meaningful ways in which the state requires its citizens to act, speak, and behave in ways that do not correspond, and even conflict, with their conscience. Indeed, Milton and Hobbes's recognition that inward freedom is intimately tied with outward behavior resonates with contemporary controversies on the public display of conscience. Spinoza and Bayle's concerns with the social and psychological implications of hypocrisy seem quite alive today as sincerity, authenticity, and integrity seem increasingly elusive in politics. The religious persecution in early modernity cannot be mapped onto the pluralistic politics of today; yet early moderns offer us now-forgotten intuitions about the negotiation of social cohesion and individual freedom that enrich our understanding of these contemporary debates.

Before I turn to Milton, it is important to acknowledge that there are limits to thinking with these figures. Recent work has challenged their received place as the great heroes in the Western canon, considering how intolerance, exclusion, and oppression are embedded in their political thought.[48] Milton was a freedom-fighter, Jeffrey Stout argues, but he was hardly egalitarian in this pursuit.[49] These revisionist accounts of early modern figures are one part of a broader conversation in the discipline of political theory on the imagining of a more inclusive canon that moves beyond the "traditional European canon."[50] The discipline of political theory should and is being reconceived as a discipline, both conceptually and methodologically, to be more inclusive, and a significant aspect of these efforts is expanding the traditional European canon to include voices and perspectives from historically marginalized intellectual traditions and communities.[51] This is essential work and as I finish this book, I am embarking on a new project on the role of dissimulation in African American political thought which, I hope, will broaden our understanding of political resistance to oppression in American politics.

---

[48] Sharon Achinstein and Elizabeth Sauer, eds., *Milton and Toleration* (Oxford: Oxford University Press, 2007).

[49] Jeffrey Stout, "Religion Unbound: Ideals and Powers from Cicero to King," Gifford Lecture Series, The University of Edinburgh, Edinburgh, UK, May 2, 2017.

[50] Melvin Rogers and Jack Turner, *African American Political Thought: A Collected History* (Chicago: University of Chicago Press, 2021), 3–4.

[51] For examples of excellent work in African American political thought, see Melvin Rogers and Jack Turner, *African American Political Thought: A Collected History*

Yet, for better or for worse, these early modern figures have shaped our modern world, and by deepening our understanding of this intellectual tradition, we arm ourselves with insights into our inherited political assumptions, intuitions, and logic, often invoked today without rigorous interrogation. Rather than try to redeem these early modern figures from charges of intolerance, I reconstruct their tolerant intuitions and acknowledge their inevitable blind spots and exclusions. Engaging with these early modern figures does not require us to embrace their views unequivocally; rather, it offers us an opportunity to learn from figures who see, more clearly than most, the psychological dynamics at stake in controversies on liberty of conscience and urge us to acknowledge and address the inevitable blind spots in our own thinking. We can also learn a great deal about ourselves by acknowledging that the received view of our inherited traditions and standard narratives about the past is not quite accurate; this exercise gives us an occasion to unsettle, revisit, rethink, and reflect on our political commitments, which are so often tied together with the stories that we tell ourselves about our past.

Now, I turn my attention to Milton who invites us to reflect on the ways that liberty of conscience is tied up with the freedom to circulate ideas in speech and writing. As Milton writes in the early pages of his revolutionary pamphlet, *Areopagitica*, books and the ideas within them are "not absolutely dead things" (CPW 2.492). By beginning this book with Milton's triumphant plea for liberty of conscience, I hope to unsettle the hostility toward liberty of conscience that dominates our current moment and remind us why this crucial – and, at the time, unsecured – liberty is so vital to our understanding of what it means to be free.

(Chicago: University of Chicago Press, 2021). For an example of excellent work on comparative political theory, see Arturo Chang, "Languages of Transnational Revolution: The 'Republicans of Nacogdoches' and Ideological Code-Switching in the U.S.-Mexico Borderlands," *Contemporary Political Theory* 21 no. 3 (2021), 373–396. For an example of excellent work on disability studies and feminist political theory, see Ann Heffernan, *Disability: A Democratic Dilemma* (forthcoming).

2 John Milton and Expressive Conscience

I MILTON'S LIBERTY "ABOVE ALL LIBERTIES"

John Milton is celebrated as one of the most spirited defenders of liberty of conscience in early modernity. In *Areopagitica*, he famously demands "the liberty to know, to utter, and to argue freely according to conscience, above all liberties" (CPW 2.560). This fervent plea for liberty of conscience emerges from Milton's condemnation of political and ecclesiastical encroachment on the dissenter. Rather than liberate conscience from infringement by religious and political authorities, the "forcers of conscience" compel conscience with financial penalties, corporal punishment, and even the threat of violent death. Religious persecution and hypocritical conformity, Milton warns, rob dissenters of the opportunity to cultivate their conscience, and in doing so, deprive them of the opportunity to cultivate the capacities of freedom. Liberty of conscience is so crucial to freedom that Milton describes it as the "highest liberty" among a broader constellation of freedoms.[1] Against "the chorus of voices vehemently defending the necessity, if not the virtue, of persecution," Milton advocates for liberty of conscience.[2]

Milton's stirring defense of liberty of conscience condemns ubiquitous early modern practices of religious persecution and hypocritical conformity. Milton's critique of book licensing refutes the widespread early modern anxiety that the loosening of print restrictions encourages religious sectarianism by allowing dissenters to "sprea[d] overt heresies and disruptive religious messages."[3]

---

[1] Stoll, *Conscience in Early Modern Literature*, 141.
[2] Walsham, *Charitable Hatred*, 49.
[3] Murphy, *Conscience and Community*, 113.

I   MILTON'S LIBERTY "ABOVE ALL LIBERTIES"   23

Proponents of religious persecution feared that the circulation of heterodox ideas would "entangle the consciences of others" by exposing them to corrupt ideas.[4] Milton's defense of liberty of conscience challenges this pervasive anxiety about the fracturing of religious uniformity and the flourishing of religious sectarianism. Religious persecution fails to compel "the inward man and his actions, which are all spiritual and to outward force not lyable" (CPW 7.254). Similarly, book licensing "conduces nothing to the end for which it was fram'd," undermining one of the most powerful early modern justifications of conformity (CPW 2.521). For Milton, hypocritical conformity does not necessarily achieve its intended goal of securing religious unity, and book licensing does not necessarily achieve its intended goal of thwarting religious sectarianism.

Despite Milton's received reputation as a champion of liberty of conscience, commentators have increasingly revised this celebratory portrait of Milton, the great hero of freedom and toleration. Stanley Fish and Abraham Stoll argue that Milton is "finally, and in a profound way, not against licensing."[5] Indeed, Fish stresses Milton's recognition of the state's interest in regulating – even censoring – seditious ideas after they have been openly circulated and scrutinized by public opinion: "I deny not, but that it is of greatest concernment in the Church and Commonwealth, to have a vigilant eye how Bookes demeane themselves as well as men; and thereafter to confine, imprison, and do sharpest justice on them as malefactors" (CPW 2.492). This broader revisionist effort to complicate the veneration of Milton, the "reassuring tolerationist," urges attention to the many "ambiguities [and] contradictions in Milton's argument[s] on toleration."[6] Sharon Achinstein and Elizabeth Sauer, for example, highlight Milton's often ignored yet indisputable exclusion of Catholics and his silence on the readmission of Jews in England in

[4] Ibid., 118.
[5] Fish, *How Milton Works*, 195; Stoll, *Conscience in Early Modern Literature*, 141.
[6] Ann Hughes, "Afterword," in *Milton and Toleration*, eds. Sharon Achinstein and Elizabeth Sauer (Oxford: Oxford University Press, 2007), 303.

24 JOHN MILTON AND EXPRESSIVE CONSCIENCE

his many writings on religious toleration.[7] Indeed, Milton excludes "Popery, and open superstition" from his defense of toleration, suggesting that Catholics cannot be tolerated because they aim to "extirpate[e]" other competing religious authorities and political sovereigns (CPW 2.565). These commentators account well for Milton's notable yet often overlooked intolerances and urge readers of Milton to reconsider his celebrated portrait as the paradigmatic theorist of toleration and freedom. To what extent does Milton's fierce defense of liberty of conscience extend beyond this minimal, exclusionary view of toleration?

This chapter argues that Milton moves beyond his acknowledgment that religious persecution is ineffective at compelling inward persuasion and suggests that hypocritical conformity threatens liberty of conscience. Building on interpretations that account well for his critique of book licensing – it is impossible to control evil books and ideas, so attempting to do so is futile – I show that Milton offers two complementary critiques of religious persecution and hypocritical conformity. First, Milton argues that they thwart the capacity for reason by eliminating opportunities for individuals to exercise their conscience. Second, Milton suggests that they harden dissenters into slavish hypocrites who engage thoughtlessly in false professions. Milton's *expressive speech* suggests that conscience must be openly and publicly expressed to be free and to protect against political disengagement. While Spinoza argues that dissenters can live blessedly despite their hypocritical conformity, Milton suggests that conformity undermines the very process through which individuals cultivate their conscience in the first place. By reconstructing Milton's defense of liberty of conscience in *Areopagitica* (1644) and *A Treatise of Civil Power in Ecclesiastical Causes* (1659), I show that

---

[7] John Coffey, "Milton, Locke, and the New History of Toleration," *Modern Intellectual History* 5, no. 3 (2008), 620. On the "intolerant" Milton, see Stanley Fish, *How Milton Works* (Cambridge, MA: Harvard University Press, 2001), 187–214; Sharon Achinstein and Elizabeth Sauer, eds., *Milton and Toleration* (Oxford: Oxford University Press, 2007), 2.

Milton's *expressive conscience* is not merely a freedom of inward conviction but an energetic, outward freedom to act in accordance with the dictates of conscience. The former focuses on book licensing, and the latter centers on religious toleration, but both pamphlets reveal Milton's deep anxiety about the thwarting of opportunities for dissenters to foster their conscience.

Such an account of *expressive conscience* foregrounds the psychological implications of Milton's view of liberty of conscience. Commentators account well for Milton's "expansive" view of liberty of conscience by highlighting the public and active implications of Milton's view of freedom.[8] Sharon Achinstein and Abraham Stoll emphasize the emergence of a public sphere and intellectual discourse to facilitate liberty of conscience,[9] and David Loewenstein stresses the importance of exercising conscience in Milton's redefinition of heresy.[10] By showcasing the expressive implications of Milton's view of liberty of conscience, I aim to complement these interpretations and reaffirm that Milton is deeply committed to free and open discourse to abate the harms done by conformity and orthodoxy. Other commentators suggest that Milton's defense of "spiritual" liberty of conscience hinges on his theology, while his "secular" defenses of the political freedoms of speech, press, and association are grounded on different premises.[11] Milton is a theorist of freedom, as many have argued, but he is also hardly a secular one. By reconstructing Milton's *expressive conscience* as implying political freedoms, even *necessitating* them, I argue that these outward freedoms do not merely derive from distinct justifications but are deeply motivated by and interwoven with Milton's defense of liberty of conscience. One of the most striking implications of Milton's *expressive conscience* is

---

[8] Stoll, *Conscience in Early Modern Literature*, 160–196.

[9] Sharon Achinstein, *Milton and the Revolutionary Reader* (Princeton: Princeton University Press, 1994), 60–65; Stoll, *Conscience in Early Modern Literature*, 160–196.

[10] David Loewenstein, *Treacherous Faith: The Specter of Heresy in Early Modern English Literature and Culture* (Oxford: Oxford University Press, 2013).

[11] Lana Cable, "Secularizing Conscience in Milton's Republican Community" in *Milton and Toleration*, 268.

its implication of a broader constellation of freedoms, such as the freedom of the press and republican liberties.[12]

Milton's account of *expressive conscience*, moreover, suggests that liberty of conscience does not merely imply an absence of constraints but also the active cultivation of cognitive capacities and the facilitation of opportunities for individuals to develop their conscience. In Milton's poetic imaginings of conscientious and unconscientious individuals, the former pursues truth with the guide of conscience – rather than religious and political authorities – and the latter is unthinking, unreflective, hardened, and dogmatic. In a world characterized by hypocritical conformity, individuals lose their opportunities to engage their liberty of conscience, and without these opportunities, individuals slowly lose the capacity to cultivate their conscience. Dissenters become hardened by their conformity and slavish to political and religious authorities; this slavishness becomes its own kind of oppression, distinct from religious persecution but still a powerful form of coercion. For Milton, religious heresy does not imply heterodoxy, but rather an unexercised conscience. By foregrounding the intellectual, cognitive, and political processes through which dissenters cultivate their conscience, Milton invites us to consider the capacities of political freedom in addition to the conditions of political freedom.

[12] On Milton's republicanism, see Nicholas von Maltzahn, *Milton's History of Britain: Republican Historiography in the English Revolution* (Oxford: Clarendon Press, 1991); Victoria Kahn, *Machiavellian Rhetoric from the Counter-Reformation to Milton* (Princeton: Princeton University Press, 1994); Quentin Skinner, David Armitage, and Armand Himy, eds., *Milton and Republicanism* (Cambridge: Cambridge University Press, 1995), especially Victoria Kahn's essay, "The Metaphorical Contact in *The Tenure of Kings and Magistrates*"; David Norbook, *Writing the English Republic: Poetry, Rhetoric and Politics, 1627–1660* (Cambridge: Cambridge University Press, 2000); Quentin Skinner, "John Milton and the Politics of Slavery," *Vision of Politics, Volume 2* (Cambridge: Cambridge University Press, 2002), 286–307; Blair Worden, *Roundhead Reputations: The English Civil War and the Passions of Posterity* (New York: Penguin, 2002); Frank Lovett, "Milton's Case for a Free Commonwealth," *American Journal of Political Science* 49, no. 3 (2005), 466–478; Quentin Skinner, *Liberty before Liberalism* (Cambridge: Cambridge University Press, 2012); Zurbuchen, "Republicanism and Toleration," in *Republicanism: A Shared European Heritage, Volume 2*, eds. Quentin Skinner and Martin van Gelderen (Cambridge: Cambridge University Press, 2002), 47–72.

II LICENSING AND BOOKS "PROMISCUOUSLY READ"

In his early pamphlet, *Areopagitica: A Speech of Mr. John Milton for the Liberty of Unlicenc'd Printing, to the Parlament of England*, Milton passionately defends liberty of conscience.[13] The title of the pamphlet gestures to the importance of outward expression, describing it as a "speech" and referencing ancient Greek oration. While the pamphlet features melodic metaphors and the cacophony of warring consciences, it is obviously a written work. This conflation of conscience and speech in the opening of the pamphlet hints at the entangled relationship between these two forms of expression and foreshadows Milton's argument that freedoms of speech, conscience, and press are intimately related.

In *Areopagitica*, Milton begins by considering the paradigm of good and evil within the object of a book. Book licensing, Milton suggests, hinges on the assumption that the regulation of written material can "suppress ... scandalous, seditious, and libelous" ideas (CPW 2.491). By limiting the circulation of these ideas, the state hopes to impede the source of sedition. Milton concedes the state's interest in regulating disunion by keeping a "viligant eye" on how "books ... as well as men ... demean themselves" (CPW 2.492). Even Milton concedes that drastic measures, such as the "confin[ing], imprison[ing], and do[ing] sharpest justice on [books] as malefactors," are justified to secure political stability (CPW 2.492). Yet Milton describes books as living creatures, setting the stage for his powerful critique of licensing as a murder of intellectual vivacity.

Milton describes books as a vessel for their author that defies the fragile constraints of mortality. Books are "not absolutely dead things," inanimate and lifeless, but are living extensions of their creators (CPW 2.492). They are active creatures – thriving and buzzing – in which authors preserve their "living intellect" (CPW 2.492). Later

---

[13] Barbara Lewalski, *The Life of John Milton* (Malden, MA: Blackwell, 2000); Blair Worden, *Literature and Politics in Cromwellian England: John Milton, Andrew Marvell, Marchamont Nedham* (Oxford: Oxford University Press, 2009).

in the passage, Milton describes books as the "precious life blood" of their authors, perhaps even more alive than their authors (CPW 2.492). Authors are "embalmed and treasured up" in their books, outliving their fragile corporeal lives (CPW 2.492). Licensing is a kind of "persecution" that destroys the "season'd life of man preserv'd and stor'd up in Books" (CPW 2.493). Milton describes licensing as a "homicide," "martyrdom," and "massacre," suggesting a kind of physical assault on ideas and their authors (CPW 2.493). Even worse than murder, it kills "immortality rather than life" by eliminating an artifact that can withstand the fragility of mortality and extend into perpetuity (CPW 2.493).

Milton expands the metaphor of books as living creatures to meat, suggesting that the seditious quality of books does not necessarily have a negative effect on its readers. Even the "best books" cannot cure a "naughty mind" of indecent thoughts, just as "wholesome meats" cannot heal a "vitiated" stomach. By arguing that evil books do not corrupt their readers, Milton challenges the justification for licensing – that evil books incite evil in their readers. Unlike rotten food which no longer nourishes the body or may even sicken it due to decay, evil books can enrich and nourish a thoughtful reader. This opportunity is crucial to cultivating conscience since an individual must be able to confront and resist evil to safeguard their conscience.

Here, Milton offers up the example of Psyche, a mortal woman who marries Eros, the God of love and sex, to illuminate the importance of the skill of distinguishing vice from virtue. In one of her four trials, Venus burdens Psyche with the impossible task of sorting a heed of "confused" and "intermixt" seeds of wheat, barley, poppy seeds, lentils, and beans (CPW 2.514). Unlike Psyche who fails at this "incessant labour," a conscientious Christian should be capable of distinguishing virtue from vice, "apprehend[ing] and consider[ing] vice with all her baits and seeming pleasures, and yet abstain[ing]" (CPW 2.514–515). The "true warfaring Christian," Milton insists, must be able to confront evil and still prefer virtue (CPW 2.514–515). Like a "good refiner" of precious metals, a conscientious reader can find gold even in the "drossiest volume" (CPW 2.521). Conscientious readers are not "defile[d]" by evil books as long as "the will and conscience be not defil'd" (CPW 2.512). Evil books, Milton insists, help a "discreet and judicious reader" by providing him with an opportunity "to discover, to confute, to forewarn, and to illustrate" (CPW 2.512–513). Victoria Kahn highlights this move in the argument, suggesting that Milton "moves from a defense of books as good or bad ... to the claim that books are things indifferent that can be used well or badly by the reader."[14] Evil books do not necessarily harm their readers but can serve as productive tools for prudent readers.

The issue of good and evil books is complicated even further in the pamphlet, inviting the reader to enlist the capacity for reasoning that Milton celebrates in the pamphlet itself.[15] While Milton begins with the dichotomy of good and evil books, he complicates this distinction by recognizing that good and evil are fundamentally "involv'd and interwoven," so much so that one cannot exist without the other (CPW 2.514). In anticipation of his retelling of the temptation of Adam and Eve in *Paradise Lost*, Milton suggests that good and evil "grow up together almost inseparably," emerging in the world as "two twins cleaving together" (CPW 2.514). Good and evil are entangled with each other, such that it is impossible to eliminate the world of evil without also eliminating virtue. Attempts to stamp evil out of the human condition, as licensing sets out to do, do not merely fail to abolish sin but also threaten to undermine virtue. By expanding the metaphor of books – from books to living creatures, to sharpening tools, to twins clinging to one another as they emerge from the womb – Milton challenges the prevailing assumption motivating book licensing – that evil can be stamped out of the human condition. By offering an account of readers untarnished by their exposure to seditious books, Milton argues that licensing laws are ineffective

[14] Kahn, *Machiavellian Rhetoric*, 175.
[15] Ibid., 175–176; Achinstein, *Milton and the Revolutionary Reader*, 4; Elizabeth Sauer, *"Paper Contestations" and Textual Communities in England, 1640–1675* (Toronto: University of Toronto Press, 2005), 30.

30 JOHN MILTON AND EXPRESSIVE CONSCIENCE

in thwarting evil and may even undermine opportunities to cultivate virtue. At first blush, Milton defends the futility of licensing to
ensure virtue in its readers; yet this view of licensing is complicated
even further since exposure to sin can enrich a dissenter by exposing
him to an opportunity to confront and resist evil. Moreover, good
and evil cannot be neatly distinguished, Milton suggests, but exist
concurrently, such that attempting to eliminate vice destroys virtue.
Even in the early pages of the pamphlet, Milton anticipates the central argument of the piece; not only does licensing fail to cultivate
virtue, but it has unanticipated and unwelcome consequences for the
virtue of dissenters.

III   THE EXERCISING OF CONSCIENCE

Not only does Milton maintain that "the order of licensing conduces
nothing to the end for which it was fram'd," but he also argues that it
harms readers by thwarting their capacity for reasoning (CPW 2.521).
The capacity for reason implies freedom, specifically the freedom
to choose, shifting the source of virtue from the objects of books to
their readers who must choose judiciously. God endows individuals
with reason, granting them the "freedom to choose, for reason is but
choosing" (CPW 2.527). The capacity for reason implies the freedom
to use that capacity. Individuals have the capacity to choose, so they
must be granted the liberty to do so. By eliminating the very possibility of choice, licensing impedes the capacity for reason. Milton does
not merely emphasize the importance of reason, but he stresses that
this capacity must be exercised continually as our ability to choose –
to differentiate good from evil – wanes without practice. The capacity for reason must be employed daily to maintain its critical edge:

> Well knows he who uses to consider, that our faith and
> knowledge thrives by exercise, as well as our limbs and
> complexion. Truth is compar'd in Scripture to a streaming
> fountain; if her waters flow not in a perpetuall progression, then
> sick'n into a muddy pool of conformity and tradition. A man

III THE EXERCISING OF CONSCIENCE 31

may be a heretick in the truth; and if he believe things only because his Pastor says so, or the Assembly so determins, without knowing other reason, though his belief be true, yet the very truth he holds, becomes his heresie (CPW 2.543).

Like "our limbs and complexion," which require daily movement to maintain their strength and health, the capacity for reason must be engaged consistently through exposure to competing ideas (CPW 2.543). Book licensing impedes this exertion by "disexercis[ing] and blunt[ing]" our ability to engage with ideas (CPW 2.491–492). This view of reason as requiring exercise suggests that the capacity for reason is not static or stable but must be practiced routinely to be maintained over time. Book licensing, Milton worries, weakens our ability to reason by eliminating one of the most important opportunities to practice the act of choosing – reading. By shifting the act of choosing from authors and readers to state licensers, individuals are robbed of a crucial opportunity to exercise their capacity for reason.

Milton's concern with the deterioration of the capacity for reason hinges on the elusive quality of truth. Like water, which must "flow in a perpetuall progression" to avoid stagnancy, truth must be contested to ward off the complacency of "conformity and tradition" (CPW 2.543). By stressing intellectual independence rather than heterodoxy, Milton offers a radical redefinition of religious heresy.[16] In contrast to the prevailing early modern view of heresy as religious sectarianism, Milton's heretic obeys political and ecclesiastical authorities. On Milton's definition, heresy is not religious dissent but unexercised conscience. Heretics do not choose for themselves but relinquish their conscience to political and religious authorities. Even a faithful dissenter who believes in "Truth" remains a heretic if

---

[16] Stephen Dobranski and John Rumrich, eds., *Milton and Heresy* (Cambridge: Cambridge University Press, 1998); Benjamin Myers, "'Following the Way Which Is Called Heresy': Milton and the Heretical Imperative," *Journal of the History of Ideas* 69, no. 3 (2008): 375–393; David Loewenstein, *Treacherous Faith: The Specter of Heresy in Early Modern English Literature and Culture* (Oxford: Oxford University Press, 2013).

32 JOHN MILTON AND EXPRESSIVE CONSCIENCE

he only believes in the truth at the suggestion of "his Pastor ... or the Assembly" (CPW 2.543). Ideas must be considered and reconsidered to ensure a free conscience. Dissenters must be free to choose for themselves and exercise their conscience; hypocritical conformity and religious dissimulation obstruct this process by urging dissenters to perform disingenuous worship and false professions. The very fact of false conformity interrupts the process through which dissenters develop and exercise their conscience. Milton's *expressive conscience* implies an energetic, active expression of conscience that is incompatible with the false and obedient expression of hypocritical conformity and religious dissimulation.

Elsewhere in his writings, Milton stresses the threat of religious conformity to liberty of conscience. In *Of Civil Power*, Milton continues to align heresy with the dogmatic obedience of external authorities. In early modernity, heresy traditionally implied the "choise or following of any opinion good or bad in religion or any other learning" (CPW 7.247). Milton redefines the conventional view of heresy as dissent, suggesting that a heretic is someone who "follows the church against his conscience" (CPW 7.248). For Milton, heresy implies the denial of conscience and obedience to religious authorities that demand conformity in their efforts to thwart sectarianism. Accordingly, Milton suggests that "he who holds in religion that beleef or those opinions which to his conscience and utmost understanding appeer with most evidence or probabilitie in the scripture, though to others he seems erroneous, can not more be justly censur'd for a heretic then his censurers; who do but the same thing themselves while they censure him for so going" (CPW 7.248). Religious dissimulation violates liberty of conscience by urging dissenters to disregard their conscience. Rather than define heresy as dissent, Milton describes it as "he who holds opinions in religion professdly from tradition" (CPW 7.252). Dissenters must submit to their conscience rather than profess – often disingenuously – the state religion, reaffirming the threat of dogma and tradition to liberty of conscience.

For Milton, Catholics are the paradigmatic example of heretics since they follow external religious authorities rather than conscience. Milton appeals to "poperie," an early modern derogatory term for Catholicism, and insists that the "papist [is] the only heretic, who counts all heretics but himself" (CPW 7.249). Milton's radical redefinition of heresy as Catholic idolatry rather than Protestant sectarianism emphasizes the dangers of dogmatic obedience to doctrine, tradition, and institutions. By "profess[ing]" an "implicit faith" in the institution of the Catholic Church and the religious figure of the Pope, Catholics place their conscience in a position of "voluntarie servitude ... to man instead of God" (CPW 7.254). By forfeiting liberty of conscience to dogma and tradition, Catholic conscience becomes submissive and obedient rather than active and energetic. After all, Milton's *expressive conscience* implies a dynamic and exercised conscience that is antithetical to religious dogmatism. Hypocritical conformity and religious dissimulation are "popish," Milton argues, suggesting that they are fundamentally antithetical to an exercised conscience. Catholic "conscience" is so obedient to religious authority that it becomes "almost ... no conscience" at all (CPW 7.254). While dogmatism is characteristic of Catholicism as Milton understands it, this account of "poperie" can be practiced by Protestants; Protestants who attempt to "force" religious conversion "deserve as little to be tolerated themselves, being no less guiltie of poperie in the most popish point" (CPW 7.254). For Milton, dogmatic obedience to religious authorities does not only undermine liberty of conscience but fundamentally alters conscience such that it no longer exists even in the first place.

IV THE "LEAST BRUISE OF CONSCIENCE"

While Milton focuses on religious toleration in *Of Civil Power*, he also addresses religious dissimulation in *Areopagitica*. After all, the debate on book licensing is entangled with the debate on religious toleration since many of the unlicensed publications concern religious sectarianism. Proponents of licensing, Milton suggests, "perpetually

34 JOHN MILTON AND EXPRESSIVE CONSCIENCE

complain of schisms and sects" (CPW 2.550). The loosening of licensing measures, critics insist, functions as a "nursing mother to sects" by nurturing religious difference and inviting "calamity" into political and social life (CPW 2.550, 452). Yet Milton turns this critique on its head, suggesting that attempts to preserve religious uniformity breed more conflict than religious sectarianism, an argument that Bayle will later affirm. Rather than "suppressing" sects, severe measures of persecution "invest [sects and schisms] with a reputation," legitimizing nascent sects even further (CPW 2.542). By showcasing the counterintuitive implications of hypocritical conformity, Milton anticipates Hobbes and Bayle's suggestion that religious dissimulation has harmful, unexpected consequences that the sovereign does not anticipate. The efforts of conformists, Milton warns, do not merely fail to inspire persuasion but can strengthen sectarianism.

Not only does hypocritical conformity embolden religious sectarianism, but efforts to undermine religious difference transform dissenters into slavish, unthinking hypocrites. Milton offers up the example of the city of London to refute the argument that religious sectarianism fractures a political community. In his iconic image of London, Milton describes "this vast City," as a "City of refuge, the mansion house of liberty" (CPW 2.554). In direct praise of Parliament, Milton traces "the immediate cause of all this free writing and free speaking" to the "mild, and free, and human government" of England (CPW 2.559). Parliament "enfranchis'd, enlarg'd and lifted up" the English people by allowing for the free circulation of ideas (CPW 2. 559). This unleashing of liberty of conscience cannot, Milton suggests, be easily reversed without enormous consequences. This freedom cannot be taken away from the English people, as doing so would make them "lesse capable, less knowing, [or] lesse eagerly pursuing of the truth" (CPW 2. 559). Milton describes this prior oppressive state as fundamentally persecutory and suggests that these coercive constraints foster ignorant, uncritical, and unenlightened individuals. The English people would be intellectually vulgar and uncritical, perhaps willing to comply and conform to the state religion, but not

IV THE "LEAST BRUISE OF CONSCIENCE" 35

in any deep or genuine way. The English people cannot go back to a state of unknowing or unfreedom after they were liberated. The English people cannot be made "ignorant, brutish, formall, and slavish," after this unleashing of freedom without using "oppressive, arbitrary, and tyrannous" measures; this would require the very measures "from whom ye have free'd us," a continuation of his effusive, albeit mocking, praise of Parliament. Hypocritical conformity shapes individuals into uncritical, unthinking individuals, such that it does not make sense to imagine a critical, conscientious dissenter who practices hypocritical conformity. Now that this freedom has been unleashed for the English people, it cannot be restricted without the reinstantiation and perhaps even intensification of extraordinarily oppressive measures.

Here, Milton offers up his famous defense of liberty of conscience: "Give me the liberty to know, to utter, and to argue freely according to conscience, above all liberties" (CPW 2.560). At first blush, Milton's defense of liberty of conscience seems like a straightforward denunciation of religious persecution and hypocritical conformity. On closer examination, however, Milton's view of liberty of conscience implies three further freedoms. First, it encompasses the freedom to "know," to cultivate conscience through the capacity for reason rather than submitting to religious dogma and institutions. Here, Milton gestures toward some degree of inward freedom – an internal, psychological, and cognitive dimension of conscience. Second, it implies the freedom to "utter," suggesting an outward freedom of expression. Dissenters should be free to cultivate their conscience *and* express that conscience without interference from the state. Lastly, it implies the freedom to "argue according to conscience," suggesting that dissenters should be free to debate with others, implying an expressive and active discourse and competing consciences in the public sphere. Milton imagines a "judicious" man "of a conscience" who must be allowed to "publish to the world what his opinion is, what his reason, and wherefore that which is now thought cannot be sound" (CPW 2.547–548). Milton's *expressive* conscience implies outward political freedoms of expression to debate and reflect collectively on truth.

Liberty of conscience extends beyond the freedom of inward conviction to an expressive freedom, suggesting that other political and outward freedoms hinge, in part, on liberty of conscience. In particular, Milton focuses on a free press since the genre of written expression facilitates open and sustained discourse. Unlike speech acts, which immediately dissipate once spoken, only to be recounted to others by witnesses, the written word persists beyond the immediate moment. This resonates with Milton's understanding of books as "living creatures" in the beginning of *Areopagitica*, an extension of authors which outlive the mortal body and allow for sustained intellectual conversation across time and place. Milton insists on liberty of conscience "above all [other] liberties," but his view of *expressive conscience* implies a broader constellation of freedom.

Milton's *expressive conscience* is not a minimal freedom of inward conviction but requires – even necessitates – outward freedoms. Not only should individuals be free to choose according to their capacity for reason, but they should also be free to express those convictions in speech and writing. For Milton, it would be illogical to suggest that a dissenter enjoys liberty of conscience, for example, if he is not granted the freedom of expression. Milton's view of the liberty of conscience directly motivates his criticism of licensing which limits the publication of written materials, wherein infringing on the conscience of both the writer and the reader. Hypocritical conformity and religious dissimulation violate liberty of conscience by asking dissenters to engage in disingenuous religious professions and curbing the cultivation and expression of conscience.

In addition to suggesting that the conformist's attempt to "crowd" conscience is ineffective, Milton stresses the harm done by hypocritical conformity to dissenters forced to comply with the state religion. This "crowding" of conscience, Milton warns, turns dissenters into hypocrites (CPW 2.551). Hypocritical conformity leads to the "forc't and outward union of cold, and neutrall, and inwardly divided minds" (CPW 2.551). While religious persecution secures the pretense of false uniformity in civil society, it simultaneously generates a society of hypocrites that are outwardly compliant and inwardly divided. In a startling visual account of oppression, Milton imagines that this "iron yoke of outward conformity" leaves a "slavish print upon our necks" (CPW 2.563–564). This description of the deformed dissenter weighed down by chains showcases the severity and burden of hypocritical conformity, hardly a minor inconvenience or innocuous display of compliance. Conformists might secure a "rigid externall formality," but this false semblance of cohesion merely reveals insincerity. Rather than coerce dissenters into genuine conversion, Milton calls for "charity of patient instruction to supple the least bruise of conscience" (CPW 2.567). This language of "bruising" reaffirms the injury done to conscience by hypocritical conformity; while this bruising is tolerable, it should be lessened to the extent possible.

Elsewhere in his writings, Milton stresses the nefarious consequences of hypocritical conformity, especially false religious sacraments and professions. In *Of Civil Power*, Milton begins by acknowledging that religious persecution fails to "beget repentance or amendment of life" (CPW 7.261). Yet Milton moves beyond the "uneffectual" use of force to stress the psychological burden of hypocrisy on dissenters (CPW 7.261). Rather than incite "honest confutation," compulsion breeds "hardness of heart, formalitic, [and] hypocrisie" (CPW 7.269). The language of "hardness of heart" describes the deadening of the spirit in the face of oppressive demands. Moreover, the language of "formalitie" implies the rigidity of ceremony and performance rather than sincere or authentic observance of religious worship. Lastly, Milton's appeal to "hypocrisie" implies a concern with the disingenuousness of outward behavior, as compelled by the state rather than demonstrative of the authentic will of the individual. In particular, Milton stresses that the compulsion of religious worship violates conscience. Individuals should not be subject to the "bondage of ... ceremonies" and "forcible imposition of those circumstances, place and time in the worship of God," freeing them from the compulsion of disingenuous religious professions and mandatory religious services (CPW 7.262). Victoria Silver highlights this concern with ceremonies and circumstances, arguing that the compulsion of religious worship violates liberty of conscience.[17] Milton also criticizes the use of fines and tithes to enforce religious conformity, describing these "injustices" as a type of "inquisition" and "violence" against conscience (CPW 7.245).

Rather than coerce conscience through corporal punishment or financial penalty, conscience should be "perswaded without scruple," allowing each dissenter to cultivate his conscience unburdened by external pressure (CPW 7.266). Attempts to compel religion by the "forcers of conscience" have not inspired genuine conversion, but have only furthered "persecutions, imprisonments, [and] banishments" (CPW 7.240). Their attempts to assume authority over conscience have led to "troubles, persecutions, commotions," all of which Milton suggests that states should avoid to curb unnecessary "bloodshed" (CPW 7.240). Bayle will echo this sociological assessment of religious persecution in his writings, insisting that persecution rather than toleration is the source of conflict. Lastly, Milton considers whether "prophane and licentious men" should be compelled in the "performance of religious and holy duties" or if they should be free to act in accordance with their "tender consciences" (CPW 7.267). Milton argues that hypocritical conformity "dishonor[s]" God by "multiplying ... sin," thereby exacerbating the heresy of religious sectarianism (CPW 7.268). The compulsion of conformity is so grave that it is "no less dangerous to perform holie duties irreligiously then to receive holy signs or sacraments unworthily" (CPW 7.268–269). Moreover, Milton challenges the assumption that one can perform an action that he does not believe in, suggesting that "if prophane and licentious persons must not neglect the performance of religious

---

[17] Victoria Silver, "Milton's Equitable Grounds of Toleration," in *Milton and Toleration*, 164.

and holy duties, it implies, that such duties they can perform; which no Protestant will confirm" (CPW 7.267). Disingenuous worship, Milton suggests, is not worship; it does not fulfill the desired goal of the "forcers of conscience" and merely reveals "popish" conformity. Milton anticipates an early modern intuition that hypocritical conformity violates liberty of conscience by robbing individuals of opportunities to cultivate their conscience and develop the cognitive and political capacities for freedom. Dissenters must be allowed to cultivate their conscience independently of religious and political authorities, and hypocritical conformity undermines this crucial process.

V CONCLUSION

By foregrounding the processes through which individuals develop their conscience, Milton urges us to reconsider the severity of the violation of hypocritical conformity and religious dissimulation. What degree of freedom does liberty of conscience imply? And how might undermining liberty of conscience threaten freedom more broadly? Milton's *expressive conscience* suggests that liberty of conscience implies constraints and capacities. First, constraints on expressions of conscience must be curtailed to allow individuals to develop and express their conscience; this continual expression of conscience is necessary to allow for the cultivation and honing of conscience. Book licensing and hypocritical conformity are not merely misguided attempts to curb evil from the human condition (impossible, after all, since evil emerges in the world, appended to virtue), but are also misunderstandings of what it means to be free in the first place. When individuals conform to the state religion, their consciences are transformed into something else – something fundamentally distinct from conscience which reflects the world around it rather than their inward persuasion. For Milton, liberty of conscience necessitates a broader constellation of freedoms – the freedom to consider, to urge, to express, to debate, and to argue – for these outward freedoms secure our inward freedom. Liberty of conscience is not static but must be protected and practiced over time. It is also not an absolute freedom. Milton places many limits on liberty of conscience – some that we may agree with and others that we may not – but he urges us to consider minimizing infringements on liberty of conscience.

For John Milton, liberty of conscience implies a broad view of freedom and the political implications that follow from it. Thomas Hobbes, on the other hand, anticipates the many threats to political stability and civil peace that liberty of conscience enables in political society. For Hobbes, hypocritical conformity does not necessarily infringe on our freedom by blunting the development of our capacities of political freedom but ensures the very foundation of political stability and civil peace that keep the political project afloat. Like Milton, Hobbes acknowledges that many dissenters are not willing to dissemble the state religion. Rather than celebrating this defiance of coercion and conformity, Hobbes proposes an educational process to cultivate conscience. Hobbes's account of *instilled conscience* invites us to consider alternative solutions to the threat of competing consciences than religious persecution and hypocritical conformity. Without an answer to the intractable threat of liberty of conscience, Hobbes warns, politics will inevitably break down into the kind of "conscience wars" that are familiar today.

3 Thomas Hobbes and Instilled Conscience

I HOBBES'S AMBIVALENCE TOWARD CONSCIENCE

Unlike John Milton, who fiercely defends liberty of conscience, Thomas Hobbes is one of its sharpest critics. Throughout his writings, Hobbes vehemently condemns liberty of conscience for empowering dissenters to disagree, disregard, and disobey their sovereigns. Hobbes's apprehension of this nascent freedom stems from his account of human conflict in the state of nature. In this "naturall condition of mankind," individuals are confronted with constant threat and insecurity, a "warre, as is of every man, against every man."[1] To overcome this state of incessant competition and evade violent death, individuals abdicate the natural freedom they enjoy in the state of nature and mutually endow a political ruler – the sovereign – with absolute authority. The promise of peace is so crucial – and the alternative so bleak – that Hobbes advocates for the restriction of freedom in exchange for stability. Even Hobbes himself acknowledges that he has been "sharply criticized on the ground that I have *taken away* liberty of conscience," corroborating the received view of the subversion of conscience in Hobbes's political thought.[2] Liberty of conscience, Hobbes cautions, threatens the sovereign's absolute authority and returns civil society back to the chaotic state of nature.

Hobbes's vitriolic position on conscience echoes the broader condemnation of conscience in early modern defenses of conformity

---

[1] Thomas Hobbes, *Leviathan*, ed. Noel Malcolm (Oxford: Clarendon Press, 2012), Volume 3, Chapter 13, 192, italics in original. Hereafter cited parenthetically as L with volume, chapter, and page number.

[2] Thomas Hobbes, *De Cive*, eds. Richard Tuck and Michael Silverthorne (New York: Cambridge University Press, 1998), 15, emphasis added. Hereafter cited parenthetically as DC with page number.

and persecution. Hypocritical conformity and absolute obedience were necessary solutions to religious conflict in a newly multiconfessional society. Hobbes's concern with the political and social repercussions of liberty of conscience reflects a pervasive anxiety among many of his contemporaries about the dangers of religious sectarianism and political heterodoxy.[3] By excusing dissenters from their obligations to the state and allowing religious sectarianism to flourish, toleration risks inciting "chaos, discord, faction, and anarchy" in civil society.[4] For Hobbes, hypocritical conformity is a solution to the inevitable chaos that "typically resulted from untrammeled conscience," which resists authority and obedience at every turn.[5] By invoking liberty of conscience, dissenters attempt to refashion themselves into sovereigns and reclaim the crucial roles of arbiter, judge, and, most problematically, legislator from the sovereign. Unlike Milton, who attends to the harms done by religious persecution and hypocritical conformity, Hobbes decries the dangers of toleration and liberty of conscience.

Despite Hobbes's received reputation for denouncing liberty of conscience, some of his readers argue that he liberates it by endowing the subjects of the Hobbesian commonwealth with a freedom of inward belief. Indeed, Hobbes famously suggests that individuals must conform to the "Publique Reason" of the sovereign in "Speech and Action," but maintains that the sovereign cannot compel the "very Thoughts, and Consciences of men" (L 3. 46, 1096). Unlike many other early modern proponents of conformity who embrace a more invasive attempt to compel inward persuasion, Hobbes accepts the futility of coercion.[6] This concession of inward freedom hinges on a psychological intuition about the futility of persecution to inspire genuine conversion; the sovereign cannot compel conscience with the threat of force as it is an internal phenomenon uncontrolled

[3] Murphy, *Conscience and Community*, 55, 12; Walsham, *Charitable Hatred*, 2, 39, 56.
[4] Murphy, *Conscience and Community*, 12.
[5] Walsham, *Charitable Hatred*, 49.
[6] Murphy, *Liberty, Conscience, and Toleration*, 249.

I HOBBES'S AMBIVALENCE TOWARD CONSCIENCE 43

by the will. The hard distinction between *forum internum* and *forum externum* has become a central interpretive puzzle for commentators committed to reconciling Hobbes's surprising liberal concession of inward freedom with his notorious absolutist and Erastian defense of political sovereignty. As Richard Tuck notes, "the question of how far Hobbes thought that a sovereign's judgments should refashion the inner life of his subjects has remained one of the most difficult issues in Hobbes scholarship."[7]

Yet commentators have complicated this revisionist account even further by showing that Hobbes is not merely preoccupied with outward conformity but also with inward persuasion.[8] Many readers of Hobbes notice that he is not merely interested in the uniformity of the *forum externum* of subjects but is also concerned with influencing the *forum internum* of the subjects of the commonwealth. The familiar view of the Hobbesian answer to the problem of plu ralism – absolute obedience and hypocritical conformity – does not sufficiently solve the problem of difference. Despite Hobbes's spirited insistence on outward conformity, Julie Cooper stresses that he still worries that "coercion ... [and] laws do not reliably produce the

---

[7] Richard Tuck, "Hobbes, Conscience, and Christianity," in *The Oxford Handbook of Hobbes*, eds. A. P. Martinich and Kinch Hoekstra (Oxford: Oxford University, 2016), 481.

[8] On Hobbes's educational project, David Johnston, *The Rhetoric of Leviathan: Thomas Hobbes and the Politics of Cultural Transformation* (Princeton: Princeton University Press, 1986); Geoffrey Vaughan, *Behemoth Teaches Leviathan: Thomas Hobbes on Political Education* (Lanham, Lexington Books, 2002); Jeremy Anderson, "The Role of Education in Political Stability," *Hobbes Studies* 16, no. 1 (2003), 95–104; Kinch Hoekstra, "The End of Philosophy (The Case of Hobbes)," *Proceedings of the Aristotelian Society* 106, no. 1 (2006), 25–62; Teresa Bejan, "Teaching the Leviathan: Thomas Hobbes on Education," *Oxford Review of Education* 36, no. 5 (2010), 607–626; Michael Krom, *The Limits of Reason in Hobbes's Commonwealth* (New York: Bloomsbury, 2013); Julie Cooper, *Secular Powers: Humility in Modern Political Thought* (Chicago: University of Chicago Press, 2013); Teresa Bejan, "First Impressions: Hobbes on Religion, Education, and the Metaphor of Imprinting," in *Hobbes on Politics and Religion*, eds. Laurens van Apeldoorn and Robin Douglass (Oxford: Oxford University Press, 2018), 45–62; S. A. Lloyd, *Ideals as Interests in Hobbes's Leviathan* (Cambridge: Cambridge University Press, 1992); S. A. Lloyd, *Morality in the Philosophy of Thomas Hobbes: Cases in the Law of Nature* (Cambridge: Cambridge University Press, 2009); S. A. Lloyd, *Interpreting Hobbes's Political Philosophy* (Cambridge: Cambridge University Press, 2019).

affective and intellectual dispositions on which they depend," such that further measures of persuasion are necessary in order to secure peace.[9] To this end, Hobbes theorizes a top-down program of civic education that aims to cultivate the inner sensibility of an obedient, peaceful subject – what Sharon Lloyd has called an "ingenious theoretical solution to the problem of disorder."[10] These interpretations offer a more nuanced account of Hobbes's concern with inward dissent, inevitably made public as outward heterodoxy. While Hobbes recognizes the inefficacy of persecution to force inward persuasion, Teresa Bejan argues that he also acknowledges that the sovereign "can and do[es] make an impact" on his subjects' inner persuasions.[11] What is the scope and target of this project of persuasion?

This chapter argues that Hobbes's sovereign does not merely aim to influence the broader *forum internum* of his subjects but, more specifically, attempts to cultivate the consciences of his subjects through civic education. Building on interpretations that account well for the sovereign's efforts to influence the inward realm of his subjects, I show that conscience, while inviolable, remains deeply subject to the sovereign's influence. Hobbes's conceptual history of conscience suggests that present-day invocations of conscience are not actually claims of conscience, properly understood, but assertions of opinion. Hobbes's account of the role of civic education in cultivating, or "gently instill[ing]" opinion implies that the sovereign can and should attempt to shape the consciences of English subjects to abate the intractable threat of liberty of conscience. Hobbes's view of *instilled conscience* suggests that conscience is reflective of external influences on the dissenter; external authorities aim to shape and cultivate conscience, raising the broader questions of where conscience comes from and what we safeguard by protecting it. By tracing Hobbes's ambivalence toward conscience alongside his account of civic education in *De Cive* (1642), *Leviathan* (1651),

[9] Cooper, *Secular Powers*, 61.
[10] Lloyd, *Ideals as Interests in Hobbes's Leviathan*, 166.
[11] Bejan, "First Impressions," 56.

I HOBBES'S AMBIVALENCE TOWARD CONSCIENCE 45

and *Behemoth, or the Long Parliament* (written in 1668, published posthumously in 1681), civic education emerges as a crucial way to confront one of the most dangerous threats to political sovereignty – liberty of conscience.

Such an account of *instilled conscience* illuminates an alternative approach to Hobbes's striking ambivalence toward liberty of conscience. Influential commentators have offered two consonant answers to the interpretive puzzle of Hobbes's seemingly contradictory position on liberty of conscience. For Alan Ryan and Richard Tuck, Hobbes concedes a minimal freedom of inward belief despite his insistence on hypocritical conformity in outward behavior.[12] Other influential commentators, such as Arash Abizadeh, Teresa Bejan, and Jeffrey Collins, expand this "liberal" interpretation of Hobbes by suggesting that he is willing to tolerate some degree of outward dissent as long as it does not interrupt the public uniformity of the worship of the commonwealth.[13] While these interpretive accounts attribute various degrees of limited toleration to Hobbes, they share an assumption about Hobbesian toleration – that Hobbes accepts difference as a fact and thus considers it the most effective way to respond to the inevitable conflicts sparked by difference. By situating Hobbes's view of toleration alongside his account of civic education, I argue that Hobbes does not merely theorize how to respond to difference but also theorizes strategies to impede difference. Hobbes is not merely a critic or proponent of liberty of conscience, as many

---

[12] Alan Ryan, "Hobbes, Toleration and the Inner Life," in *The Nature of Political Theory*, eds. David Miller and Larry Seidentop (Oxford: Clarendon Press, 1983), 197–218; Alan Ryan, "A More Tolerant Hobbes?" in *Justifying Toleration: Conceptual and Historical Perspectives*, ed. Susan Mendus (Cambridge: Cambridge University Press, 1988), 37–60; Richard Tuck, "Hobbes and Locke on Toleration," in *Thomas Hobbes and Political Theory*, ed. Mary Dietz (Lawrence, KS: University of Kansas Press, 1990), 153–171; Tuck, "Hobbes, Conscience, and Christianity," 579–601.

[13] Arash Abizadeh, "Publicity, Privacy, and Religious Toleration in Hobbes's *Leviathan*," *Modern Intellectual History* 10, no. 2 (2013), 261–291; Jeffrey Collins, *Allegiance of Hobbes* (Oxford, Oxford University Press, 2005), 1–10, 123–124, 102–109, 129–135, and 253–254; Teresa Bejan, "Difference without Disagreement: Rethinking Hobbes on 'Independency' and Toleration," *Review of Politics* 78, no. 1 (2016), 1–25; Bejan, *Mere Civility*, 96–97, 101.

have argued, but also a theorist of the solution to the problem of conscience.

This account of *instilled conscience*, moreover, showcases one of the key targets of Hobbes's educational efforts – liberty of conscience. Influential commentators on Hobbesian education account well for the ways that Hobbes's sovereign cultivates peaceful, obedient subjects. Sharon Lloyd and Teresa Bejan focus on the "formal features" of education, while Julie Cooper offers a more robust account of the "peculiar content" of the state curriculum.[14] Once we pay closer attention to Hobbes's conceptual understanding of conscience – specifically his understanding of the third view of conscience as opinion – we are in a better position to appreciate the extent to which this broader educational effort specifically targets liberty of conscience. Hobbes's educational project aims to secure civil peace, and one of the most important ways to abate political conflict is by reeducating the Hobbesian commonwealth on the proper understanding of conscience.

By theorizing civic education as an effort to reeducate conscience, Hobbes invites us to reflect on whether the sovereign can overcome the threat that difference poses to the commonwealth once and for all. If conscience can be properly cultivated by the sovereign through civic education, then we might read Hobbes as optimistic that the intractable problem of conscience will eventually be if not resolved, then at least abated. If conscience can be properly cultivated, the sovereign will not have to demand hypocritical conformity or concede a limited degree of toleration but can aim for a world in which such considerations wane. If civic education is effective at instilling conscience, as Hobbes hopes, dissenters will not view their conscience as conflicting with the sovereign. They will embrace, rather, a kind of "knowing with" the sovereign. But before we consider Hobbes's solution to the intractable problem of liberty of conscience, it is essential to begin with his conceptual history of conscience and condemnation of liberty of conscience.

[14] Lloyd, *Morality in the Philosophy of Thomas Hobbes*, 338.

II HOBBES'S CONCEPTUAL HISTORY OF CONSCIENCE

Before reconstructing Hobbes's familiar absolutism, on the one hand, and his puzzling concession of inward freedom, on the other, it is instructive to begin with Hobbes's definition of conscience in *Leviathan*.[15] In Chapter 7, "Of the Ends, or Resolutions of DISCOURSE," Hobbes offers a conceptual history of conscience which features three distinct views of the phenomenon:

> When two, or more men, know of one and the same fact, they are said to be CONSCIOUS of it one to another; which is as much as to know it together. And because such are the fittest witnesses of the facts of one another, or of a third; it was, and ever will be reputed a very Evill act, for any man to speak against his *Conscience*; or to corrupt, or force another so to do: Insomuch that the plea of Conscience, has been alwayes hearkened unto very diligently in all times. Afterwards, men made use of the same word metaphorically, for the Knowledge of their own secret facts, and secret thoughts; and therefore it is Rhetorically said, that the Conscience is a thousand witnesses. And last of all, men, vehemently in love with their *own new opinions*, (though never so absurd,) and *obstinately bent to maintain them*, gave those their opinions also that reverenced name of Conscience, as if they would have it seem unlawfull, to change or speak against them; and so pretend to know they are true, when they know at most, but that they think so (L 2.7, 100, emphasis added).

Hobbes's first account of conscience describes it as a kind of knowledge through which "two, or more men, know of one and the same fact" together. This experience of shared knowledge is described as being "CONSCIOUS of it one to another" (L 2.7, 100). Conscience is an experience of shared knowledge through which secrets are revealed; it is the faculty through which the concealed is made

---

[15] On *Leviathan* as a more reverent work than *De Cive* toward conscience, see Jeffrey Collins, *Allegiance of Hobbes* (Oxford, Oxford University Press, 2005), 123–124.

48 THOMAS HOBBES AND INSTILLED CONSCIENCE

known. Hobbes expands on the experience of shared knowledge with the metaphor of the witness, suggesting that individuals who are "conscious of it one to another" function as a kind of witness to one another, even "the fittest witnesses of the facts of one another" (L 2.7, 100). Hobbes seems amenable to this first view of conscience, even suggesting that it is conscience properly understood. In the second definition of conscience, Hobbes transitions to a "metaphorical" view of conscience as shared knowledge of "secret facts, and secret thoughts," and a "thousand witnesses" (L 2.7, 100).[16] Hobbes's use of the metaphor of the witness here is crucial.[17] Conscience operates as a kind of witness to our inner thoughts and convictions, like a testimony to our deepest yearnings and desires that would otherwise be obscured to external observers. Conscience is not necessarily discernable through outward actions that make inward conscience known; rather, conscience itself is the faculty through which this knowledge is facilitated.

Finally, Hobbes introduces a third view of conscience as opinion, arguing that contemporary invocations of conscience are not appeals to conscience but "new opinions (though never so absurd)" that men are "obstinately bent" on "maintain[ing]" (L 2. 7, 100). This description of conscience as opinion, we can glean from Hobbes's preceding definitions of science and opinion, implies a lack of proper knowledge and misguided conclusions, ungrounded in the proper understanding of definitions. Dissenters invoke the "reverenced

---

[16] On Hobbes and metaphor, see Bryan Garsten, *Saving Persuasion: A Defense of Rhetoric and Judgment* (Cambridge, MA: Harvard University Press, 2006), 42; Rebecca Ploof, "The Automaton, the Actor and the Sea Serpent: Leviathan and the Politics of Metaphor," *History of Political Thought* 39, no. 4 (2018), 634–661.

[17] "Witness, n.," *Oxford English Dictionary Online*, accessed September 17, 2018, www.oed.com/view/Entry/229713?rskey=XTALJ4&result=1. The Oxford English Dictionary offers several definitions of witness, such as a kind of "knowledge, understanding, and wisdom," or relatedly, an "attestation of a fact, event, or statement," definitions which will be more familiar to modern readers. However, Hobbes employs an early modern view of witness which implies the "inward testimony of the conscience," as traced to Corinthians. This definition of "witness" as related to conscience appears broadly in early modernity, e.g. Shakespeare's *Merry Wives of Windsor* (1623): "May we with ... the witnesse of a good conscience."

II HOBBES'S CONCEPTUAL HISTORY OF CONSCIENCE   49

name of Conscience" to disguise and legitimize acts of disobedience since it would be inexcusable to "change or speak against" conscience (L 2.7, 100). Dissenters downgrade, Hobbes argues, the status of the revered phenomenon to mere opinion. This third view of conscience anticipates Hobbes's familiar hostility toward conscience; contemporary invocations of conscience are not claims of conscience but assertions of opinion which undermine obedience to the sovereign and incite civil conflict.

Recent scholarship, however, has set out to challenge the "liberal" interpretation of Hobbes as endorsing liberty of conscience by returning to his seemingly contradictory view of conscience in the puzzling first and second views of conscience in this conceptual history.[18] Johan Tralau and Mark Hanin suggest that the first view of conscience as "being conscious" with others stresses the surprising "collective" and "social" quality of conscience. This first view of conscience, they suggest, would require the toleration of dissenting outward behavior to facilitate shared knowledge – a recognition that liberty of conscience is not achieved by securing a minimal freedom of inward conviction. Yet the toleration of dissenting forms of religious worship and association, they note, would pose an unacceptable threat to the Hobbesian commonwealth. Liberty of conscience would interrupt religious uniformity and introduce social disorder, so these commentators speculate that Hobbes must not have meant to endorse it. For Tralau and Hanin, Hobbes's puzzling view of collective conscience is evidence that readers of *Leviathan* should be skeptical of any endorsements of liberty of conscience in its pages.

Situating Hobbes's conceptual history of conscience in the early modern discourse of casuistry, however, reveals that Hobbes is not necessarily endorsing a public or collective view of conscience. In particular, Hobbes's first view of conscience as "knowing with others" does not necessarily imply a more robust understanding of

---

[18] Johan Tralau, "Hobbes Contra Liberty of Conscience," *Political Theory* 39, no. 1 (2010), 15; Mark Hanin, "Thomas Hobbes's Theory of Conscience," *History of Political Thought* 33, no. 1 (2012), 55–85.

50   THOMAS HOBBES AND INSTILLED CONSCIENCE

toleration but is reflective of conventional metaphors for conscience in the seventeenth-century discourse on casuistry, a discourse with which he would have been familiar from his studies at Oxford. As Abraham Stoll suggests, "many familiar details from the discourse of conscience can be found" in Hobbes's account of conscience.[19] Hobbes describes conscience as shading into consciousness, as a witness, and as knowing with – all conventional views of conscience in the seventeenth-century discourse on casuistry.[20] Hobbes's third account of conscience as opinion, however, deviates significantly from conventional early modern understandings of conscience, suggesting that the familiar view of Hobbes's hostility toward conscience as "absurd opinion" cloaked in the name of "conscience" still stands.

III THE "SEDITIOUS" DOCTRINE OF LIBERTY OF CONSCIENCE

Hobbes's hostility toward liberty of conscience does not only appear in his conceptual history of conscience but features prominently throughout his writings. In the examination of potential sources of dissolution of the commonwealth in *De Cive*, Hobbes asserts that the liberty of conscience is the most "seditious" political doctrine imaginable in a civil society (DC 131). The "private men" of the commonwealth who appeal to conscience to justify dissent are not behaving as dutiful subjects but are "aspiring to be ... Kings" of their state (DC 132). These agitators undermine the commonwealth by attempting to reclaim the authority that they had previously transferred to the sovereign in the social contract. This "seditious" doctrine is so dangerous that Hobbes asserts that 'tender' conscience is "without question" the most poignant threat a commonwealth can face (DC 131). The corrosive repercussions of conscience can hardly be overstated, as Hobbes recognizes that "when this happens the commonwealth cannot stand" (DC 132). Hobbes's hyperbolic engagement with liberty of conscience suggests that liberty of conscience

[19] Stoll, *Conscience in Early Modern English Literature*, 92–93.
[20] Ibid., 93.

III   THE "SEDITIOUS" DOCTRINE OF LIBERTY OF CONSCIENCE   51

is so poisonous that it will inevitably destroy a commonwealth, a rather loaded warning to sovereigns to limit the role of conscience in political and social life.

Hobbes offers a similar account of the threat that the liberty of conscience poses to the political stability of the commonwealth in *Leviathan*. In Chapter 29, "*Of those things that Weaken, or tend to the DISSOLUTION of a Common-wealth,*" Hobbes offers his most infamous criticism of liberty of conscience as a meaningful threat to sovereignty. The subversive doctrine that "*every private man*" should be his own "*Judge of Good and Evill actions,*" emboldens each dissenter to act on his own judgment of moral considerations rather than obey the law of the commonwealth (L 2.29, 502, emphasis in original). While each individual maintains this right of judgment in the "condition of meer Nature," this right is transferred to the sovereign, the "Judge, the Legislator," once the individual enters into the social contract (L 2.29, 502). Liberty of conscience undermines the commonwealth by fracturing sovereignty.

In this account, Hobbes's concern with this rebellious impulse seems motivated by a recognition of the inevitable chaos inspired by mere difference.[21] Individuals are driven by competing "Appetites, and Aversions," which depend largely on their "different tempers, customes, and doctrines," explaining the wide diversity of viewpoints and perspectives (L 2.15, 242). These differences, moreover, endanger the commonwealth by provoking individuals to "dispute [and disobey] the commands of the Common-wealth" when they differ from their own opinions (L 2.29, 502). Dissenters will not "obey the Soveraign Power, farther than it shall seem good in [their] own eyes," but will act in accordance with their opinions (L 2. 29, 502). This intractable individual judgment inevitably leads to "Disputes [and] Controversies," and in its most radical iteration, "War" (L 2.15, 242). Respect for liberty of conscience, Hobbes insists, is therefore

---

[21] On the sources of disagreement for Hobbes, see Arash Abizadeh, "Hobbes on the Causes of War: A Disagreement Theory," *American Political Science Review* 105, no. 2 (2011), 298–315; Bejan, *Mere* Civility, 85–91.

52 THOMAS HOBBES AND INSTILLED CONSCIENCE

"repugnant to Civill Society," for it encourages disobedience (L 2.29, 502; emphasis in original). Political stability is so important, and the threat of conscience so dangerous that Hobbes diligently warns of its pernicious consequences.

IV THE FUTILITY OF COERCION

While received accounts focus on Hobbes's severe insistence on hypocritical conformity, Hobbes does concede a degree of inward freedom that many other prominent Erastian and Anglican writers and preachers did not. Rather than defend the much harsher and more invasive position of inward-directed persecution, Hobbes places limits on the sovereign's coercive reach over the *forum internum* of subjects. Indeed, some of Hobbes's contemporaries worried that he was too lenient on conscience, a surprisingly contradictory view of Hobbes's stance on liberty of conscience. Samuel Parker, for example, fervently attacked *Leviathan* for the "Consequences that some men draw from Mr. Hob's Principles *in behalf* of Liberty of Conscience."[22] If liberty of conscience is such a "seditious" doctrine – one of the most meaningful threats to political sovereignty – why is Hobbes also accused of defending it? Perhaps Hobbes's contemporaries were right to treat Hobbes, at least comparatively, as a proponent of liberty of conscience.

The concluding chapters of *Leviathan* stress the inviolability of the inward realm. In Chapter 37 of *Leviathan*, "Of Miracles and their Use," Hobbes tackles the contested topic of the possibility of miracles in the present-day, an important issue given the ubiquity of claims of religious enthusiasm. There, Hobbes insists that subjects of the commonwealth must accept the judgment of the sovereign, "Gods Supreme Lieutenant," to whom they have "submitted our private judgments" rather than follow their "own private Reason, or Conscience" (L 3.37, 696). On the tail end of this endorsement of obedience, however, Hobbes offers a surprising concession: "A private

---

[22] Richard Tuck, "Hobbes and Locke on Toleration," 167, emphasis added.

IV THE FUTILITY OF COERCION 53

man has alwaies the liberty, (because thought is free), to beleeve, or not beleeve in his heart" (L 3.37, 696). The metaphorical representation of the heart suggests that inward conviction is both uncontrollable by external forces and opaque to the external observer; the heart remains both impenetrable against compulsion and obscure to outward interrogation. While action *can* be coerced with constraint or threat, thought is uniquely free since it is both inaccessible to the sovereign and incoercible with force. The sovereign cannot compel men either to believe or not believe; the heart, as the metaphoric representation for our inner conscience, remains impenetrable.

This view appears elsewhere in *Leviathan*. In Chapter 40, "Of the Rights of the Kingdome of God...," Hobbes adds that subjects must "obey the laws of [his] Sovereign, in the externall acts and profession of Religion" (L 3.40, 738). But, the "inward *thought*, and *beleef* of men, which humane Governours can take no notice of," should not lie in the sovereign's jurisdiction "for God onely knoweth the heart" (L 3.40, 738). Belief is not "voluntary," nor the result of the "effect of the laws" but "of the unrevealed will, and of the power of God" and as such, "fall[s] not under obligation" to the state (L 3.40, 738). In his discussion of ecclesiastical authority, Hobbes adds that "Faith hath no relation to, nor dependence at all upon Compulsion, or Commandement; but onley upon certainty, or probability of Arguments drawn from Reason, or from something men beleeve already" (L 3.42, 782). As such, the "Ministers of Christ in this world, have no Power by that title, to Punish any man for not Beleeving, or for Contradicting what they say," refuting the coercion of conscience by political and ecclesiastical authorities (L 3.42, 782). This concession is, however, limited to inward belief. The sovereign can "lawfully Punish any Contradiction to their laws whatsoever," which would have hardly satisfied Puritans who were invoking liberty of conscience to justify their dissent from the sovereign's laws (L 3.42, 782). Unlike outward behavior which men can control, matters of "Beleef, and Unbeleef never follow mens Commands," suggesting that inner conviction lies outside of the scope of the sovereign's coercive reach (L 3.42, 784). Given that faith is outside of our control, methods of persecution, including the "promise of rewards, or menaces of torture," are not successful (L 3.42, 784). Attempts to compel persuasion, Hobbes insists, will only be futile.

Hobbes's familiar hostility toward conscience seems undermined by his puzzling endorsement of the inviolability of interiority and even conscience itself. On the one hand, Hobbes condemns liberty of conscience for undermining sovereignty, and, on the other hand, he stresses the limits of the sovereign's coercive reach to compel conscience. Commentators have accounted well for two approaches to this interpretive puzzle: on the one hand, claims of "tender" conscience corrode sovereignty and invite political and religious strife; but on the other hand, the sovereign cannot curb conscience with force. To what extent can the sovereign protect against abuses of conscience given Hobbes's acknowledgment of the futility of coercion? Are there alternative ways to deal with the problematic consequences of conscience in politics? Hobbes does not merely attempt to confront the intractable problem of conscience with repressive demands for hypocritical conformity, or liberate conscience as long as it does not interrupt "publique" uniformity, but also theorizes complementary methods of education and persuasion to tame "tender" consciences. Hobbes's ensuing engagement with civic education, accordingly, is motivated by his concern with competing claims of conscience and the threat they pose to politics. Civic education, we will see, helps abate the threat of liberty of conscience, shifting conscience from opinion to "knowing with" the sovereign.

V   INSTILLED CONSCIENCE AND CIVIC EDUCATION

By reconstructing Hobbes's ambivalence toward conscience and highlighting the limits of the efficacy of hypocritical conformity, civic education emerges as a powerful way to address the intractable problem of conscience in politics. In particular, Hobbes's recommended educational agenda aims to challenge the prevailing view of conscience in early modern England, the third view of conscience

V INSTILLED CONSCIENCE AND CIVIC EDUCATION 55

offered in Hobbes's conceptual history of conscience. By "rooting out" certain opinions and "gently instilling" others, the sovereign reeducates the consciences of his subjects, detaching them from their view of conscience which encourages dissenters to disobey the sovereign and instilling a view of conscience as a kind of "knowing with" the sovereign.

For Hobbes, the task of reeducating conscience is central to securing centralized sovereignty. The ubiquity of claims of "tender" conscience in early modern England is, at its core, indicative of the pervasiveness of divided sovereignty. Those who assert their "tender" consciences are not obedient to conscience, properly understood, but are merely submissive to a competing sovereign; after all, what Puritan dissenters are really saying when they assert their "tender" consciences is that they are obedient to another sovereign. Their "tender" consciences have not been properly cultivated through a "knowing with" God or their fellow subjects but reflect the efficacious education of "competing sovereigns." In particular, Hobbes traces the origins of the third view of conscience to universities and pulpits, two sources of education which must be redirected by the sovereign toward civil peace and stability. The universities and preachers, rather than the sovereign, have been spearheading civic education, thereby functioning as competing sovereigns in society. Hobbes's proposal for civic education is aimed at securing peace more broadly, and it does so by reeducating conscience.

For Hobbes, education is of central importance because hypocritical conformity is not sufficient to secure political and social stability. Opinion breeds outward disobedience, so education is necessary to cultivate inward uniformity. Even in his early writings, Hobbes argues that the sovereign must try to influence his subjects' opinions through civic education since "every man's actions are *governed by his opinions*" (DC 80, emphasis added). The language of governance stresses the crucial impact of inward heterodoxy on outward disobedience; opinion ultimately determines outward behavior. In *Leviathan*, Hobbes continues to connect the project of influencing opinion with securing obedience, recognizing that the "Actions of men proceed from their Opinions; and in the wel governing of Opinions, consisteth the well governing of mens Actions" (L 2. 18, 272). Hobbes reiterates the deep connection between action and opinion, such that inward dissent provokes correspondingly outward heterodoxy. Opinions are crucial to political stability, Hobbes insists, because they shape outward behavior. Hobbes is even more explicit about the political stakes of this connection in *Leviathan* – the governance of inward opinion entails the governance of outward behavior. Hypocritical conformity does not succeed in securing uniformity since dissenters will not actually comply in practice; rather, the sovereign must set out to influence his subjects' inward realms to achieve civil peace since it is only through the governance of inward belief that the sovereign can secure outward compliance. This argument can hardly be overstated as it complicates the standard view of Hobbes; on the received view, Hobbes demands hypocritical conformity but is uninterested in inward coercion. Yet Hobbes concedes a psychological resistance to hypocritical conformity – dissenters will not willingly comply because acting at odds with their conscience is quite burdensome.

The sovereign's educational agenda also features prominently in Chapters 18 and 30 of *Leviathan*. In Chapter 18, "*Of the* RIGHTS *of Soveraignes by Institution*," Hobbes begins to describe the foundational goals of civic education. The sovereign must adjudicate which "*Opinions* and *Doctrines*" are "averse" and "conducing" to Peace and restrict the promotion of those ideas accordingly (L 2.18, 272, italics in original). In particular, Hobbes is interested in the promulgation of the "deeply rooted" opinion that is "contrary to the peace of Man-kind," that "man shall Judge of what is lawfull and unlawfull ... *by their own Consciences*," reiterating his critical position on the liberty of conscience (L 2.18, 272, emphasis added). He targets the promotion of liberty of conscience in writing, suggesting that the sovereign should "examine the Doctrines of all bookes before they be published," endorsing the very kind of licensing policies that Milton

V INSTILLED CONSCIENCE AND CIVIC EDUCATION 57

wrote against so fervently in *Areopagitica* (L 2.18, 272). The sovereign should not only determine which opinions are detrimental to the stability of the commonwealth but also manage the dissemination of those opinions by limiting his subjects' exposure to seditious ideas.

The sovereign must accordingly cultivate specific opinions to secure outward uniformity. Civic education, or "publique Instruction, both of Doctrine, and Example" must be "diligently, and truly" overseen by the sovereign (L 2. 30, 520, 522). This educational agenda is two-pronged, requiring both the promotion of certain opinions and the thwarting of others. The sovereign must decide which "*Opinions* and *Doctrines*" are "averse" and "conducing" to the "Defence, Peace, and Good of the People," cultivating the latter and impeding the former (L 2.18, 272; 2. 30, 520, italics in original). The "common people" must be "diligently instructed in the true principles of their duty," especially since they do not know "right of wrong by their own meditation" (B 70–71, 144). Not only do they need to learn about their obligations to the state, but they must also be helped to see "the reasons why calamities ... follow disobedience to the lawful sovereigns" (B 144). Hobbes warns, moreover, that this two-part process must be gentle rather than forceful:

> It is therefore a duty of those who administer sovereign power to root these doctrines out of the citizens' minds *and gently instil others*. But as opinions are sown in men's minds *not by command but by teaching*, not by threat of penalties but by clarity of argument, laws to resist this evil should be directed not against the people in error but against the errors themselves (DC 146–147, emphasis added).

First, civic education requires the unsettling of certain opinions, represented with the image of expunging; this process of "rooting out" evokes the image of a weed, frustratingly burrowed in the ground. This "rooting out" process is necessary to allow for the success of the sovereign's educational agenda since pernicious opinions are already widespread; English subjects are hardly like "clean paper, fit to receive whatsoever by Publique Authority shall be imprinted in them" but are covered with an array of scribbles and scrawls that reflect competing allegiances to alternative sovereigns (L 2.30, 524).[23] Subjects have been previously educated by competing sovereigns, so the sovereign must first untether subjects from their tightly held opinions. By challenging the "weeds of error and superstition," the sovereign can ensure that his subjects are open to his educational agenda.[24]

This "rooting out" process, on closer examination, is specifically aimed at conscience. In particular, Hobbes argues that the sovereign must target the "deeply rooted" idea of liberty of conscience – that each "man shall Judge of what is lawfull and unlawfull ... by their own Consciences" (L 2.18, 272). The most important idea which must be rooted out of subjects' minds is the third view of conscience, suggestive of the underlying relationship between Hobbes's vitriolic position on conscience and his advocacy for civic education. The qualifier of "deeply rooted" suggests that this view of conscience has largely dominated the early modern imagination, as entrenched as it is ubiquitous – a pessimistic assessment of the status of conscience in English society. The invocation of "judge," moreover, reaffirms Hobbes's condemnation of this view of conscience as a violation of sovereignty; subjects are attempting to reclaim important roles of authority which belong to the sovereign. The conflation of conscience with opinion must be stamped out of the minds of English subjects to make way for the proper understanding of conscience as a kind of "knowing with," a forgotten view of conscience which Hobbes flags in his conceptual history of conscience.

The process of "rooting out" is crucial, Hobbes insists, given how tightly dissenters cling to their erroneous opinions. By encouraging his readers to be more critical, more discerning, and ultimately

---

[23] On the metaphor of "imprinting" in Hobbes's account of civic education, see Bejan, "First Impressions," 45–62.

[24] Johnston, *The Rhetoric of Leviathan*, 191.

V INSTILLED CONSCIENCE AND CIVIC EDUCATION 59

more obedient to the "true" sovereign, Hobbes aims to unsettle the conscience of his readers to make way for the impact of civic education. This "deflationary strategy" introduces the slightest hint of doubt to make dissenters question their consciences.[25] Are you sure your conscience is guided by divine inspiration? Is it possible that you have erred? Or that those who claim divine inspiration have erred themselves or are, even worse, lying? This technique is not coercive, but it remains deeply effective, Hobbes hopes, in changing the minds of subjects.

One key target of this deflationary strategy is contemporary invocations of prophecy, many of which Hobbes suggests are misguided or even worse, fraudulent. Many alleged prophets claim to have "spoken to God," but they are merely imagining this encounter. While some prophets claim to have "spoken to [God] in a Dream," this is merely to say that "he dreamed that God spake to him" (L 3. 32, 580). This is hardly demonstrative of divine inspiration. Dreams "proceed from former thoughts," so a dream-like vision is reflective of one's musings rather than a real experience of "extraordinary Revelation" (L 3. 32, 580). These dreams are demonstrative of "selfe conceit, and foolish arrogance, and false opinion of" their own "godlinesse" (L 3. 32, 580).[26] Others claim to have "seen a Vision, or heard a Voice," but these individuals are merely in a state between "sleeping and waking" (L 3. 32, 580). These alleged prophets, Hobbes warns, are either misjudging their dreams or even more nefariously, flat out lying: "who (being a man) may erre, and (which is more) may lie" (L 3. 32, 580). This approach encourages dissenters to be "circumspect, and wary, in obeying the voice of man, that pretending himself to be a Prophet," encouraging dissenters to be more vigilant (L 3. 36, 674). By untethering dissenters from their hasty loyalties, this "rooting out" process makes way for gentle instruction and the proper cultivation of conscience.

[25] On Hobbes's deflationary project, see Alison McQueen, *Political Realism in Apocalyptic Times* (Cambridge: Cambridge University Press, 2018), 143–144.

[26] On Hobbes's critique of vainglory, see Cooper, *Secular Powers*, 48–50, 61.

This "rooting out" process is subsequently complemented by the "gentl[e] instilling" of subjects of the commonwealth. Hobbes does not embrace the repressive invasion of the interiority of subjects "with command," but advocates for gentle "teaching" (DC 146). The Oxford English Dictionary offers two related definitions of "instill," both traced to John Milton.[27] The first definition implies the process of "introduc[ing] by little into the mind, soul, heart," or "to infuse slowly or gradually," suggestive of the educational process that Hobbes describes in *De Cive* – slow, subtle, and measured.[28] Hobbes's use of "instilling," however, aligns even more closely with Milton's use of the term in *Of Education*, in which instilling means "to imbue with" through measures of education. The qualifier of "gentle," moreover, implies that these efforts should be mild and tempered rather than severe and coercive; this education should be grounded on reason, or "clarity of argument" rather than force, or "threat of penalties," surprisingly akin to the measured form of persuasion advocated by Milton.

Hobbes's advocacy for gentle instruction is puzzling, especially given his penchant for absolutism. Why not embrace the repressive compulsion of dissenters' interiority? Severe forms of coercion which aim to coerce interiority, Hobbes argues, tend to backfire against the sovereign. Hobbes appeals to the puzzling distinction between *forum internum* and *forum externum* in *Behemoth*, explaining that attempts to compel conviction are not merely futile but incendiary:

> A state can constrain obedience, but convince no error, nor alter the minds of them that believe they have the better reason. Suppression of doctrine does but unite and exasperate, that is, increase both the malice and power of them that have already believed them.[29]

---

[27] "Instill, v.," *Oxford English Dictionary Online*, accessed September 17, 2018, www.oed.com/view/Entry/97076?redirectedFrom=instill#eid.

[28] Lloyd, *Ideals as Interests in Hobbes's Leviathan*, 162.

[29] Thomas Hobbes, *Behemoth, or Long Parliament*, ed. Ferdinand Tönnies (Chicago: University of Chicago Press, 1990), 62.

V INSTILLED CONSCIENCE AND CIVIC EDUCATION   61

While the sovereign can enforce hypocritical conformity with the threat or use of force, attempts to compel conviction with violence risk intensifying seditious opinions. Not only are these attempts futile – they fail to successfully "convince" subjects of specific opinions – but they further attach subjects to their zeal. The "suppression" of sedition actually convinces dissenters of their conscience even more. Like Milton, Hobbes recognizes the psychological obstacles to hypocritical conformity; yet instead of exploring the way that it hardens the dissenter, he argues that it emboldens religious fervor and dissenters' attachment to their consciences. Hypocritical conformity has the exact opposite effect of its intended goal. Rather than enlisting force to influence subjects' interiority, Hobbes advocates for the gentle instilling of his subjects' inward persuasions, abating the risk of aggravating dissent. This gentle approach to persuasion is central to the sovereign's efforts since more aggressive approaches threaten to undermine the sovereign's very objective of educating his subjects. Gentle measures of education, rather than violent measures of persecution, are the most promising paths to civil peace.

Hobbes's account of civic education in Chapter 30 of *Leviathan* begins with advising against certain doctrines that threaten to undermine political stability and absolute authority, while also instilling others that promote civic peace and secure sovereignty. In particular, Hobbes stresses several doctrines which the subjects of the commonwealth must be taught *not* to follow, suggesting the broader problem that the English people have already been educated in pernicious ways. The metaphor of the blank page highlights the extent to which Hobbes's educational program is concerned with unlearning as much as instilling. Individuals must be taught "not to be in love with any forme of Government they see in their neighbour Nations," or to "desire change," in political regime, as this envy might lead to political instability or attempts at rebellion (L 2. 30, 524). Individuals must also be taught "not to be led" to venerate specific individuals in the commonwealth, as their deep affection for other leaders might undermine their allegiance to the sovereign (L 2. 30, 526). In an effort to further secure the authority of the sovereign, Hobbes adds that individuals must be "informed, how great a fault it is, to speak evill of the Sovereign," restraining potential challenges to sovereign authority (L 2. 30, 526). In Chapter 30, Hobbes also explores the "Means, and Conduits," of these lessons, such as civic ceremonies in which subjects "assemble together" and "hear ... their Duties ... read and expounded," suggestive of the importance of recurrent instilling (L 2. 30, 528). This broader educational program is fundamentally concerned with political obedience to the sovereign, so it is not surprising that Hobbes quickly turns to one of the most important threats to obedience and authority – liberty of conscience. In stark contrast to Hobbes's account of civic education, the universities and religious preachers have improperly educated the English people – especially by promoting the pernicious idea of liberty of conscience. To secure political peace and social stability, the sovereign must dismantle this third dangerous view of conscience as opinion.

VI COMPETING SOVEREIGNS, COMPETING CONSCIENCES

Sovereignty hinges on the centralization of education, in part, because Hobbes recognizes that competing sovereigns have largely dominated public edification in early modern England. Hobbes's recommendation for civic education is then not merely an abstract proposal but a pragmatic agenda grounded in a recognition that competing sovereigns have overwhelmingly directed the broader education of the English people and promoted divided allegiances. By enlisting the language of "instilling" in his consideration of the "Divines in the Pulpit" and the faculty "of discoursing readily, and plausibly" at universities, Hobbes draws attention to their dangerous – and largely successful – educational efforts. The universities and churches, Hobbes argues, are the two key channels through which seditious opinions – especially liberty of conscience – have "come to be instilled into the People" (2.30, 532). Rather than teach men about "their duty" to obey the sovereign, Hobbes warns that these competing sovereigns have preached "rebellion and treason"

VI COMPETING SOVEREIGNS, COMPETING CONSCIENCES 63

(B 39). Elsewhere, Hobbes laments the role of "preaching friars" in "instilling" obedience to the Catholic Church, reiterating the role of clergy in cultivating divided allegiances (B 15–16). The language of "instilling" echoes Hobbes's intimations in *De Cive* on the potential influence of sovereign authorities to influence the inner theater of their subjects.

Commentators have accounted well for Hobbes's condemnation of these sources of civil conflict, stressing their role in inciting the English Civil War.[30] In particular, Hobbes traces the origins of the third view of conscience as mere opinion to universities and pulpits, two sources of education which must be redirected by the sovereign toward civil peace and stability. The proper "education of ordinary people in their civic and moral duties," as Lloyd notes, would require the prior instruction of "preachers trained in correct doctrine in the universities."[31] The universities are the breeding ground for both the clergymen and the "learned men," and as the presumed origins of sedition, they are central to Hobbes's project of sovereignty. Hobbes emphasizes university reform accordingly: "The Instruction of the people dependeth wholly, on the right teaching of the Youth in the Universities" (L 2.30, 532). The possibility of the proper education of the people is first predicated on university reform, so much so that Hobbes views "reforming the universities … [as] necessary to the maintenance of perpetual stability."[32]

Hobbes reiterates this theme in *Behemoth*, stressing that universities are especially problematic since "all [of the] preachers proceeded" from the Universities" (B 41). Preachers are effective,

---

[30] On the role of universities in the English Civil War, see Bejan, "Teaching the *Leviathan*," 607–627; Bejan, "First Impressions: Hobbes on Religion, Education, and the Metaphor of Imprinting," 49–58; Krom, *The Limits of Reason*, 127–161; Vaughan, *Behemoth Teaches Leviathan*, 42; Richard Tuck, "Hobbes on Education," 152–154; Collins, *Allegiance of Hobbes*, 35; Lloyd, *Ideals as Interests in Hobbes's Leviathan*, 197–220; Jon Parkin, "Hobbes and the Future of Religion," *Hobbes on Politics and Religion*, eds. Laurens van Apeldoorn and Robin Douglass (Oxford: Oxford University Press, 2018), 197–220.

[31] Lloyd, *Ideals as Interests in Hobbes's Leviathan*, 274.

[32] Ibid., 161.

64 THOMAS HOBBES AND INSTILLED CONSCIENCE

Hobbes warns, in "draw[ing] the people to their opinions," especially their disdain for "Church-government, Canons, and the Common-prayer-book" (B 23). Unlike Milton who argues that writing is more important than preaching since the spoken word effectively dissipates after the current moment passes, Hobbes recognizes the power of the spoken word. For him, both "sermons and writing" are both deeply persuasive and powerful over people (B 24). Not only do sermons provoke dangerous opinions, but they have the potential for wide-spread reach; preachers have a substantial audience – even wider than the literate public of England who can read Scripture independently – allowing them to preach sedition to the English people.

To this end, commentators have further considered the substantive sources of Hobbesian education. Many commentators, such as Teresa Bejan, note Hobbes's "maligned" suggestion that *Leviathan* should serve as the "basis of the university curriculum" for these reformed universities.[33] Yet the suggestion that *Leviathan* "would make a suitable university text" is not a fully developed curriculum.[34] As Quentin Skinner teases, Hobbes's self-endorsement "hardly amounts to a syllabus."[35] While Hobbes is less specific than his readers might reasonably expect given the importance of civic education, university reform is central to the Hobbesian project of consolidated sovereignty. Educated at universities, preachers are also significant since they are effectively bridges to the broader public through proselytization. Preachers have a substantial audience, even wider than the literate public of England, allowing them to preach sedition widely through sermons. As Vaughan stresses, "the role of

---

[33] Bejan, "First Impressions: Hobbes on Religion, Education, and the Metaphor of Imprinting," 49; Tuck, "Hobbes on Education," 154; Jon Parkin, "Hobbes and the Future of Religion," 200; Lloyd, *Ideals as Interests in Hobbes's Leviathan*, 274.

[34] Lloyd, *Ideals as Interests in Hobbes's Leviathan*, 274.

[35] Quentin Skinner, *From Humanism to Hobbes: Studies in Rhetoric and Politics* (Cambridge: Cambridge University Press, 2018), 189. Julie Cooper explores some of the additional resources that Hobbes proposes, such as the Book of Job, to educate the Hobbesian subject "in the virtues of modesty" beyond *Leviathan*. Cooper, "Vainglory, Modesty, and Political Agency in the Political Theory of Thomas Hobbes," 245.

VI COMPETING SOVEREIGNS, COMPETING CONSCIENCES 65

Puritan preachers in the Civil War must not be forgotten."[36] The sovereign must accordingly thwart the educational efforts of these two powerful competing sovereigns in order to secure peace.

Commentators have accounted well for Hobbes's condemnation of universities and preachers as provoking civil conflict, but less attention has been given to their role in cultivating conscience. In particular, Hobbes traces the third view of conscience – conscience as mere opinion – to the "tongues, and pens of unlearned Divines," an especially damning critique of the dangerous doctrines spread by universities and preachers (L 2.29, 504). Not only have these competing sovereigns been largely successful in their efforts to incite the English people, but they are the source of the problematic conflation of conscience with opinion recounted in his conceptual history of conscience. These competing sovereigns have been dangerous educators of conscience, inspiring the very zealous assertions of "tender" conscience which bred civil disorder in the English Civil War.

This account of Hobbesian education raises the important question of whether "Hobbes thought that a future shaped by his ideas might develop," or more specifically, whether civic education might be effective at consolidating sovereignty and thwarting competing sovereigns.[37] How optimistic is Hobbes that education can obviate the problem of conscience in political life? At times, Hobbes seems rather cynical that the sovereign can reeducate dissenters: "The seditious doctrine of the Presbyterians has been stuck so hard into the people's heads and memories ... that I fear the commonwealth will never be cured" (B 57). On the other hand, if there is a solution to the instability afflicting early modern England, it is surely the proper education of "well-principled preachers" at "disciplined" universities: "I think it is a very good course, and perhaps the only one that can make our peace amongst ourselves constant" (B 59). If conscience

---

[36] Vaughan, *Behemoth Teaches Leviathan*, 42.

[37] On the possibility of transformation for Hobbes, see Jon Parkin, "Hobbes and the Future of Religion," 184; Johnston, *The Rhetoric of Leviathan*, 191; Lloyd, *Ideals as Interests in Hobbes's Leviathan*, 163.

is properly cultivated by the sovereign, then it seems like there will not be conflicting claims of "tender" conscience asserted against the laws of the commonwealth. The sovereign will not have to demand hypocritical conformity but can expect a proper alignment between the publique "Conscience" of the sovereign and the private consciences of each individual subject. After all, assertions of "tender" conscience are not genuine assertions of conscience, properly understood, but demonstrative of competing allegiances to other sovereigns, which will slowly disappear as subjects are properly educated. The extent to which Hobbes was optimistic about the possibility of the obviation of the view of conscience as opinion ultimately hinges on the success of the sovereign's educational project.

Despite Hobbes's suggestion that conscience can be reeducated, there are limits to the efficacy of this gentle instruction. While civic education should result in a "significant thinning of the ranks of fools, dupes, and zealots," Hobbes remains concerned with the education of ambitious men who, despite the sovereign's best efforts, might still defy the commonwealth.[38] Rather than acquiesce to the laws of the commonwealth, "there are those who believe they know better than other people, and more fit to govern than the present ministers," and these ambitious types will try to demonstrate their endowments by challenging the sovereign (DC 148).[39] These ambitious types will not "digest ... any thing that setteth up a Power to bridle their affections," making it difficult to fashion them into submissive subjects (L 2. 30, 524). Rather than attempt to intimidate ambitious types into acquiescence – in vain, no less – sovereigns should enlist a system of "rewards and punishments" that would allow for these types to secure esteem and status within the system of the sovereign state (DC 148). Some dispositions, Hobbes stresses, cannot be curbed even

---

[38] Lloyd, *Morality in the Philosophy of Thomas Hobbes*, 337.

[39] For a critical account of the possibility of Hobbes's educational system to successfully tame ambitious types, see Jeremy Anderson, "Role of Education in Political Stability," 103; Maryam Qudrat, "Confronting Jihad: A Defect in the Hobbesian Educational Strategy," *Hobbes Today: Insights for the 21st Century*, ed. S. A. Lloyd (Cambridge: Cambridge University Press, 2012).

by education; political stability requires alternative paths to allow these ambitious types to aggrandize themselves without fundamentally disrupting the commonwealth.[40] These ambitious men need, as Hobbes suggests, a different kind of education grounded on prestige and hierarchy.

VII CONCLUSION

By diagnosing conscience as mere opinion, Hobbes invites us to reflect on the very source of conscience in the first place. Where does our conscience come from? Who shapes conscience, and how do they shape it? Hobbes's *instilled conscience* shows that conscience reflects the external influence on inward persuasion. Civic education emerges as one of the most powerful ways to overcome the intractable problem of conscience. If contemporary invocations of conscience are reflective of dueling allegiances to competing sovereigns but can be instilled so as to be obedient to the one true sovereign, then the problem of conscience can be resolved, or at least abated. Perhaps hypocritical conformity cannot make good on its pledge to secure uniformity, but civic education provides a promising path forward – mild enough to avoid inciting further zeal but effective enough to impede difference.

Civic education provides a promising strategy, Hobbes argues, to break with contemporary understandings of conscience and return to earlier views of conscience. Conscience is, properly understood, a kind of "knowing with" the sovereign, to return to Hobbes's conceptual history of conscience. Civic education emerges as a way to return to this kind of "knowing with" the sovereign by promoting a "publique" conscience. If Hobbes's recommended proposals for civic education are successful, the subjects of the commonwealth will be "knowing with" one another and their sovereign. If their sovereign is legitimate, of course, then they will also be "knowing with" God. For Hobbes, conscience is one of the most meaningful threats to

[40] Lloyd, *Morality in the Philosophy of Thomas Hobbes*, 337–339; Jeremy Anderson, "Role of Education in Political Stability," 103.

sovereignty and stability; yet civic education is a powerful strategy to confront the threat of "tender" conscience afflicting his world. Even Hobbes who is known for endorsing draconian measures of hypocritical conformity and absolute sovereignty recognizes the psychological backlash incited by religious persecution, such that he advocates for more gentle measures of persuasion to ensure peace and stability.

For Thomas Hobbes, liberty of conscience is a problem that can be solved with civic education. Yet Baruch Spinoza argues that even civic education cannot overcome the intractable issue of division in the human condition. Claims of "tender" conscience are not demonstrative of abuses of power, as Hobbes suggests, but are reflective of the reality of human difference given that individuals fundamentally disagree about shared facts. For Spinoza, politics should not be concerned with eliminating competing claims of conscience but with managing inevitable conflicting consciences. Spinoza does not share Hobbes's concern that dissenters will not willingly comply with the state; rather, he argues that, even if they do conform, the state will be undermined by a lack of civic trust. Like Hobbes, Spinoza worries that liberty of conscience undermines sovereignty, yet he also acknowledges that hypocritical conformity undermines the social foundation of civil society – trust. Spinoza's account of *conscientious speech* aims to offer a compromise between limiting and liberating conscience by delineating different domains of outward behavior that can be dictated by conscience to assure this crucial precondition for toleration and freedom. Without liberty of conscience, Spinoza argues, dissenters will not know whether they can trust that their neighbor's outward behavior reflects their inward conscience, undermining the very fabric of civil society.

4 Baruch Spinoza and Conscientious Speech

I SPINOZA'S HOBBISM

While Thomas Hobbes infamously defends absolute sovereignty and condemns liberty of conscience, Baruch Spinoza has long enjoyed a reputation as the "founder of liberal democracy"[1] and a "great defender of freedom of conscience."[2] Throughout his writings, Spinoza argues for the free cultivation and expression of conscience. In *Theological-Political Treatise*, Spinoza suggests that the dissenter "should be granted the right to think what he wants and to say what he thinks," liberating him from the coercive reach of political and ecclesiastical authorities.[3] Each individual should be granted, Spinoza suggests, "the power to interpret the foundations of faith according to his own mentality," demonstrative of the importance of religious conscience in Spinoza's broader project of defending the freedom to philosophize (TPT II. 73). Hypocritical conformity threatens to undermine freedom, corroborating the received view of Spinoza as an advocate for toleration and liberty of conscience.

Spinoza's condemnation of religious persecution and hypocritical conformity, commentators argue, is rooted in his Jewish heritage and the severe repression of religious minorities, especially Jews and Muslims, across Europe.[4] As a descendent of Portuguese Marranos, a

---

[1] Julie Cooper, "Freedom of Speech and Philosophical Citizenship in Spinoza's Theologico-Political Treatise," *Law, Culture, and the Humanities* 2, no. 1 (2006), 91.

[2] Julie Henry, "Freedom of Conscience in Spinoza's Political Treatise: Between Sovereign Limitations and Citizen Demand," *Reformation and Renaissance Review* 14, no. 1 (2012),10.

[3] Baruch Spinoza, *The Collected Works of Spinoza, Volume 2*, ed. and trans. Edwin Curley (Princeton: Princeton University Press, 2016), 353. Hereafter cited in parenthetical citations at TPT with volume and page number.

[4] Yirmiyahu Yovel, *Spinoza and Other Heretics, The Marrano of Reason* (Princeton: Princeton University Press, 1992); Yirmiyahu Yovel, *The Other Within: The Marranos;*

69

Jewish community that was forced to convert to Catholicism, Spinoza understood the complicated ways that religious dissenters navigated their persecutory conditions. Many Jews were massacred, and others fled the Iberian Peninsula for more tolerant territories; most endured forced conversions while continuing to practice Judaism privately in their own homes "out of a cautious fear of persecution."[5] The forced baptism of Jews led to varying degrees of hypocritical conformity, from the full-fledged false performance of religious sacraments to partial cultural assimilation to Christianity.[6] Some "willingly adopted Christianity, and rose to high positions in the church ... to protect [other] Jews," while others "secretly donated money to a synagogue or sent oil for its ceremonies ... because of pangs of conscience."[7] Despite these varying practices of dissimulation, many Jews conformed to Catholicism outwardly while "maintaining their own [religious] beliefs in secret," creating a society in which individuals were forced to grapple with widespread suspicion that the worship of others in their community was insincere, at best, or subversive, at worst.[8] Many Jews embraced hypocritical conformity to survive persecutory conditions, but this did not eliminate suspicion. Unlike Hobbes, who defends hypocritical conformity to protect stability and sovereignty, Spinoza condemns the widespread practice of hypocritical conformity, which forced Jews to live a double life.

Yet a closer examination of Spinoza's political thought reveals that his received reputation as the "supreme philosophical bogeyman," an epithet that the intellectual historian Jonathan Israel has assigned him, must be qualified.[9] In recent years, many commentators,

---

Split Identity and Emerging Modernity (Princeton, NJ: Princeton University Press, 2009). For an interpretation of Spinoza that moves beyond his Marranism, see Steven Smith, *Spinoza, Liberalism, and the Question of Jewish Identity* (New Haven, CT, Yale University Press, 1997).

[5] Smith, *Spinoza, Liberalism, and the Question of Jewish Identity*, 19.

[6] Kaplan, *Divided by Faith*, 294–330.

[7] Yovel, *The Other Within*, 60.

[8] Kaplan, *Divided by Faith*, 157.

[9] Jonathan Israel, *Radical Enlightenment: Philosophy and the Making of Modernity 1650–1750* (Oxford: Oxford University Press, 2002), 159.

I SPINOZA'S HOBBISM 71

such as Susan James, Justin Steinberg, Michael Rosenthal, and Julie Cooper, have highlighted Spinoza's striking Hobbism, specifically his penchant for intolerance, his preoccupation with the corrosive implications of difference, and his endorsement of an all-powerful sovereign who reigns over the political arena with absolute authority.[10] For Hobbes and Spinoza, obedience to the sovereign must be unconditional, even if conscience conflicts with the law. While individuals retain freedom of inward judgment, Spinoza accepts a fairly Hobbesian concession that dissenters must "always ... *act* according to [the sovereign's] decree alone," insisting on absolute obedience in outward behavior (TPT II. 74, emphasis added). Liberty of conscience, Spinoza worries, endows each individual with the "license to *do anything*," posing an insurmountable threat to the stability of the state (TPT II. 295, emphasis added). Each individual hopes to "act solely according to the decision of his own mind," rather than obey the sovereign (TPT II. 347). By elevating conscience over the sovereign, dissenters attempt to "divide sovereignty," or even more dangerously, subsume the sovereignty of the state and fashion themselves into alternative sovereigns (TPT II. 333). Religious dissenters might express frustration about the constraints placed on their outward conduct, but Spinoza insists that dissenters must comply with the sovereign's decrees to secure stability, even if their conformity violates their conscience. Spinoza's Hobbism is also corroborated by his reception among his contemporaries. As Steven Smith emphasizes, "from virtually the moment the *Treatise* was published, [Spinoza] was excoriated as ... a Hobbesian."[11] Despite his longstanding reputation as a proponent of liberty of conscience and religious

---

[10] Susan James, *Spinoza on Philosophy, Religion, and Politics: The Theologico-Political Treatise* (Oxford: Oxford University Press, 2012); Justin Steinberg, "Spinoza's Curious Defense of Toleration," in *Spinoza's "Theological-Political Treatise": A Critical Guide,* eds. Yitzhak Melamed and Michael Rosenthal (Cambridge: Cambridge University Press, 2010); Michael Rosenthal, "Spinoza's Republican Argument for Toleration," *Journal of Political Philosophy* 11, no. 3 (2003); Julie Cooper, "Freedom of Speech and Philosophical Citizenship," 91–93.

[11] Smith, *Spinoza, Liberalism, and the Question of Jewish Identity,* 49.

72 BARUCH SPINOZA AND CONSCIENTIOUS SPEECH

toleration, Spinoza has far more in common with Hobbes than he does with Milton.

The interpretive tension between Spinoza's familiar liberalism and his recently recovered absolutism is complicated further, however, by his defense of free speech, a perplexing endorsement of *outward* freedom. Spinoza, like Hobbes, might insist on outward conformity, full stop, given the dangers of dissent. After all, outward displays of heterodox expression – public, exposed, and blasphemous – risk inciting civil disorder. Yet Spinoza does not merely protect the inward freedom to "think what [one] wishes," but also advocates for the expressive freedom "to say what [one] thinks" (TPT II. 353). What motivates Spinoza's puzzling endorsement of outward freedom? Or put otherwise, why is Spinoza ultimately not a good Hobbesian, despite his recognition of the dangers of dissent?

This chapter argues that Spinoza foregrounds the importance of conscientious expression in the cultivation of civic trust. By charting Spinoza's diagnosis of religious dissimulation in a relatively neglected passage in Chapter XX of the *Treatise*, I argue that his defense of liberty of conscience is shaped by his concern with the deleterious effects of the distrust propagated by the "pervasive and even overwhelming reality" of hypocritical conformity across early modern Europe.[12] On Spinoza's account, a society of hypocrites cannot cultivate the necessary foundation of trust to foster relationships and ensure a stable, free republic. In a world characterized by enforced conformity, individuals cannot trust that others' outward expressions reflect their genuine inner convictions, wherein breeding mistrust and thwarting freedom. Spinoza's *conscientious speech* suggests that individuals must be able to speak publicly in accordance with the dictates of their conscience, or else others will incessantly mistrust that their outward behavior reflects their inward persuasion. Spinoza defends the right of individuals to speak in accordance with the dictates of their conscience, not merely because the state is incapable of enforcing hypocritical

---

[12] Zagorin, *Ways of Lying*, 255.

I SPINOZA'S HOBBISM 73

speech but also to abate the corrosive effects of coerced expression on social relationships. By attending to the significance of sincerity and the socially corrosive consequences of enforced conformity in the *Theological-Political Treatise* (1670), hypocrisy and distrust emerge as underlying impetuses for his defense of liberty of conscience.

By demonstrating that the politics of hypocrisy lie at the center of Spinoza's defense of liberty of conscience, this chapter challenges the received view of Spinozist toleration as grounded solely on the futility of coercion. Commentators with competing methodological and theoretical commitments consistently frame Spinoza's defense of toleration as "prudential," grounded in a recognition of the limits of state power rather than a principled respect for the individual or the sanctity of conscience.[13] Jonathan Israel stresses the inefficacy of coercion, acknowledging that the sovereign cannot "control the thoughts of someone else" through force, so he should not try to do so.[14] Like Israel, Steven Smith recognizes that Spinoza's account of the freedom of judgment is not grounded on "some sacred or privileged sphere of individual privacy," but on the limits of state power.[15] Ronald Beiner also draws attention to the futility of the compulsion of conscience, suggesting that there is "no point in trying to discipline belief," given the "futility of trying to coerce the inner judgments of the mind."[16] This scholarly consensus on Spinoza's prudential defense of toleration is surprisingly sweeping, a rare moment of interpretive accord among otherwise richly diverse accounts. Of course, this argument figures prominently in the *Treatise*, in which Spinoza advocates for the freedom of judgment, in part because "what can't be prohibited must be granted" (TPT II. 348). By highlighting the limits of the sovereign's power to compel conscience, commentators account well

[13] Steinberg, "Spinoza's Curious Defense of Toleration," 210; Rosenthal, "Spinoza's Republican Argument for Toleration," 320.

[14] Jonathan Israel, *Enlightenment Contested: Philosophy, Modernity, and the Emancipation of Man, 1670–1752* (Oxford: Oxford University Press, 2006), 158.

[15] Smith, *Spinoza, Liberalism, and the Question of Jewish Identity*, 24.

[16] Ronald Beiner, "Three Versions of the Politics of Conscience: Hobbes, Spinoza, Locke," *San Diego Law Review* 47, no. 3 (2010): 1009, 1116.

for one of the underlying justifications for Spinozist toleration. Yet I show that Spinoza's defense of liberty of conscience moves beyond the futility of coercion; it is not merely that coercion does not work but that it would not reflect genuine conversion even if it seems to work. The duplicity and dissimulation inherent in hypocritical conformity threaten freedom by making individuals distrustful of those around them in civil society.

This account of *conscientious speech* invites us to consider the balancing act inherent in the politics of conscience. Like Milton, Spinoza recognizes the dangers of hypocritical conformity, but like Hobbes, Spinoza acknowledges the dangers of liberating conscience altogether. Dissenters must be free to express themselves to others, but that freedom also risks eroding the rule of law and political sovereignty. Spinoza offers an arguably surprising compromise between Milton's impassioned plea on behalf of conscience and Hobbes's vitriolic critique of conscience; he defends the freedom of *conscientious speech* yet demands obedience to the law, even if that obedience conflicts with conscience. Individuals must be able to assess whether their neighbor is friend or foe, and hypocritical conformity impairs this calculus. By foregrounding the social and psychological repercussions of the decision to liberate or coerce conscience, Spinoza urges us to reflect on the question of the impact of coercion long after the immediate moment of persecution.

II CONFORMITY, PLURALISM, AND AUTHORITY

Spinoza offers up a striking hypothetical of religious uniformity, but it is essential to situate his defense of *conscientious speech* in his surprising defense of consolidated sovereignty in Chapter XX of the *Treatise*. Just one chapter earlier, Spinoza worried about the many dangers of liberty of conscience. Chapter XIX is, as Ronald Beiner suggests, a "decidedly Hobbesian chapter," as Spinoza defends the state's authority over outward expressions of religious piety.[17] By asserting

---

[17] Ronald Beiner, *Civil Religion: A Dialogue in the History of Political Philosophy* (Cambridge: Cambridge University Press, 2010), 140.

that the sovereign must have the right to adjudicate "sacred matters" regarding the "external practice of Religion," Spinoza assigns ecclesiastical authority to the state (TPT II. 332). Elsewhere, Spinoza recommends that the sovereign be endowed with the "supreme right to maintain whatever it judges concerning religion," an endorsement of absolute authority over religion (TPT II. 295). The state is imbued with the right to "distinguish what is permissible and what is not" in matters of religious affairs, a rather robust acknowledgment of authority over the "sacred" (TPT II. 328). Like Hobbes, Spinoza stresses the supreme authority of the state over religious affairs in order to thwart the divisive consequences of religious sectarianism and protect the "peace of the Republic" (TPT II. 332). The sovereign, Spinoza argues, should oversee the religious affairs of the state, a far cry from Milton's, albeit limited, distinction between religion and politics in *Of Civil Power*.

Spinoza's endorsement of Erastianism is paired with a recognition of the importance of absolute obedience. Like Hobbes, Spinoza grapples with the harmful consequences of difference. While the sovereign should extend the freedom of judgment to his subjects, dissenters are nonetheless "bound to obey" the sovereign's commands (TPT II. 295). In the state of nature, individuals enjoy absolute freedom, but each individual acquiesces a certain degree of liberty to the sovereign in order to secure the stability and advantage provided by a consolidated authority. On Spinoza's account, it is unreasonable that individuals should expect absolute, unrestricted freedom in a political society, as this kind of limitless liberty is only characteristic of the state of nature. While absolute freedom might seem appealing to the extent that each individual is allowed to behave however he pleases, this volatility incites the very kind of disorder that inspired individuals in the state of nature to relinquish some degree of their natural autonomy for the security provided by political organization. Any acquiescence to tender conscience, Spinoza argues, inevitably leads to the "downfall of the state," by allowing individuals to disobey the law (TPT II. 347). By insisting on the sovereignty of conscience, individuals divide authority between the state and conviction and, in their more radical attempts, subsume the authority of the sovereign.

Obedience to the sovereign, therefore, must be absolute. While individuals retain freedom of judgment and speech, they must also "always ... *act* according to [the sovereign's] decree alone," insisting on absolute obedience in outward conduct (TPT II. 74, emphasis added). Liberty of conscience, Spinoza worries, endows each individual with the "license to *do anything*," a significant undermining of authority and an insurmountable threat to the authority of the state (TPT II. 295, emphasis added). Each individual hopes to "act solely according to the decision of his own mind," rather than obey the command of the sovereign (TPT II. 347). Elsewhere, Spinoza suggests that each individual must obey the sovereign "absolutely," even if this conformity infringes on their conscience (TPT II. 288). In particular, Spinoza stresses the conformity of outward behavior, what he describes as the "exercise of piety" and the "external practice of religion," which must respect the sovereign's command in order to assure the "peace and preservation" of the state (TPT II 333; 336). While inward manifestations of piety, the "internal worship of God," or the "means by which the mind is disposed, internally, to worship God wholeheartedly," are free, the outward expressions of piety should be regulated by the state (TPT II. 333). On Spinoza's account, individuals must comply absolutely with the sovereign's decree to avoid civil chaos.

This absolute obligation to the state might seem to violate the freedom of its subjects, turning them into slaves who are bound to the whims of their sovereign. Indeed, Spinoza suggests that many religious dissenters insist that they should be allowed to act in accordance with their "own heart," rather than acquiesce to the commands of the sovereign (TPT II. 288). Yet Spinoza argues that freedom is not grounded on a lack of external constraints but is concerned with the loosening of prejudice and irrationality.[18] Here, Spinoza echoes Milton in his redefinition of heresy and urges individuals to resist dogmatic obedience.

---

[18] Smith, *Spinoza, Liberalism, and the Question of Jewish Identity*, 134–136.

III THE CHALLENGE OF CONFORMITY 77

While some might complain about the constraints placed on external conduct by the state, Spinoza suggests that individuals do not necessarily maintain the unlimited freedom enjoyed by the state of nature, even in a free democracy. While Spinoza advocates for the freedom of judgment, this respect for conscience does not imply an inviolable respect for the capacity of conscience as expressed in outward conduct. For Spinoza, freedom implies liberation from the constraints of dogma; it is a kind of psychological and intellectual phenomenon.

The politically salient question then becomes whether a dissenter can be forced to act "contrary to religion," if commanded by his sovereign (TPT II. 294). On this question, Spinoza introduces a vibrant example of religious persecution: Christian tradesmen and missionaries living abroad in Japan are forced to comply outwardly with Japanese law, which forbids Christianity. The historical realities of Christian missionaries in Japan were complex, as the Tokugawa Shogunate, the Japanese government, banned Catholicism and expelled all Christian missionaries by the mid-seventeenth century. Many Christians went into hiding, practicing privately in concealed rooms in private homes, complying with the religion of the state while continuing to practice their faith secretly. Spinoza embraces the Hobbesian answer to this dilemma, suggesting that Christians must obey the Japanese law even if conformity encroaches on their conscience. While Christians cannot worship freely in outward displays of piety in Japan, Spinoza argues that they can nonetheless live "blessedly" (TPT II. 147). The inward persuasion of the individual remains aligned with conscience despite the hypocritical conformity of outward behavior. Thus far, Spinoza embraces a rather Hobbesian position on hypocritical conformity, insisting that the conscience of the dissenter is not violated despite their enforced conformity.

III THE CHALLENGE OF CONFORMITY

The importance of obedience is complicated, however, by man's predilection for defiance. Spinoza stresses a crucial obstacle to securing absolute obedience and outward conformity – dissenters are not keen on giving it. This does not necessarily seem to be an issue with general obedience to the laws, which individuals are more or less willing to obey; however, it presents a particular challenge with conscience. Dissenters are aggravated by laws that conflict with their conscience as this dissonance suggests that their conscience is erroneous. Rather than cooperate with the sovereign's commands, for example, Christian missionaries in Japan would be frustrated by the compulsion to conform to the state religion. This aggravation is so severe, Spinoza suggests, because individuals are "constituted to endure nothing with greater impatience than that the opinions they believe to be true should be considered criminal and that what moves them to piety toward God should be counted as wickedness in them" (TPT II. 349). The language of "greater impatience" stresses that dissenters are antagonized by this dissonance. Dissenters will not experience hypocritical conformity as a benign request by the state but will be offended; this perceived insult to their conscience is experienced as a serious affront that inspires individuals to break the law.

The importance of absolute obedience is complicated even further by a recognition of the inevitability of a pluralism of "opinions" and the variability of "judgment" among individuals, specifically in matters of religion (TPT II. 346). Grounded in Spinoza's view that the "mentality" of men is "extremely variable," he emphasizes that individuals naturally come to radically different views (TPT II. 346). The human experience, according to Spinoza, is fundamentally characterized by difference, even when individuals encounter shared experiences. For example, one person might be moved to religious conviction by one provocation, whereas another will be moved to laughter by the same stimulus, affirming the sweeping pluralism of the human condition. Individuals come to different views and judgments, even concerning the most important matters, ensuring that civil society is characterized by deep differences.

For Spinoza, this pluralism becomes salient in political life as individuals insist that others act in accordance with their conscience.

This insistence incites conflict as each individual hubristically assumes the validity of his opinion and, accordingly, expects others to embrace his judgments. Each individual supposes that he has a superior understanding of what is "fair or unfair, permissible, or impermissible," and so hopes to impose his view on others (TPT II. 299). Spinoza's recognition of the sheer diversity of opinions, as well as an acknowledgment of the egoism of individuals, points toward an inevitable tension across competing persuasions. Based on Spinoza's account of pluralism, it is inevitable that individuals will disagree; this disagreement will incite conflict since individuals will be frustrated by their failed attempts to convince others of their judgments. This recognition of the predilection for persuasion explains the evangelical project of Christian missionaries; they want to spread their religious faith, and complying with the law of Japan is directly at odds with that goal. Based on the recognition of the inevitability of pluralism, it seems impossible for a tolerant, and therefore, pluralistic, society to thrive.

Thus far, it would seem as though Spinoza shares many of Hobbes's intolerances, specifically his insistence on the Erastian subjugation of ecclesiastical affairs to state authority, as well as his defense of absolute obedience to the sovereign in outward conduct. Spinoza is also deeply worried about difference and the effects of difference on civil stability. Yet Spinoza differentiates himself from his absolutist contemporaries by placing significant limits on the sovereign's authority and defending the boundaries of freedom for the individual, specifically the liberty of conscience and speech. Given Spinoza's concerns with the divisive implications of difference and his rigorous defense of absolute sovereignty, the concessions of freedom in Chapter XX are a puzzling way to conclude the *Treatise*. Indeed, Spinoza could have resisted the allure of liberty and insisted on the conformity of outward expression and dissenting speech altogether. Why then does Spinoza defend liberty of conscience despite his recognition of the threat it poses to stability and sovereignty?

IV HYPOCRISY, "GOOD FAITH," AND CONSCIENTIOUS SPEECH

By tracing Spinoza's defense of *conscientious speech* and the subsequent freedom of speech that emerges from his defense of liberty of conscience, hypocrisy and distrust emerge as central concerns. In particular, Spinoza argues that dissenters must be able to speak freely in accordance with the dictates of conscience to ensure that each member of society can trust, to some degree, their neighbors. Without free expression, the very foundation of civil society – trust – cannot be cultivated, wherein thwarting the very stability that proponents of persecution seek in the first place.

Spinoza's defense of *conscientious speech* begins with his recognition of the prior, seemingly more minimal, freedom of judgment. Despite his endorsement of the sovereign's authority over outward expressions of piety, Spinoza insists that each individual remains sovereign over his convictions as he is "his own master [of] the internal worship of God" and "his own thoughts" (TPT II. 333, 345). While each individual transfers his "right to act according to his own decision," to the sovereign, he maintains the right of inward persuasion, or the "right to reason and judge" (TPT II. 333, 345). No individual can "surrender" his freedom of judgment, as each is "master of his own thoughts" (TPT II. 345). The recurring use of the language of mastery in Spinoza's defense of free judgment stresses each individual's untransferable sovereignty over his inward convictions. While each individual in the commonwealth "surrenders ... his right to *act* according to his own decision," he nonetheless retains his "right to reason and judge" (TPT II. 345). Liberty of conscience cannot be relinquished entirely to the state, even if the outward behavior that reflects that conscience can be curbed. While Christians in Japan could worship privately in their own minds or family homes, they could not express that devotion publicly. Individuals are free to believe whatever they like, Spinoza suggests, but they cannot *act* on those beliefs.

The central justification for this freedom is an acknowledgment of the inefficacy of compulsion. Rather than persuasively shape his

IV HYPOCRISY, "GOOD FAITH," AND CONSCIENTIOUS SPEECH 81

subjects' inner theater, the sovereign would "act in vain if he commanded a subject to hate someone ... or to love someone ... or not to be offended by insults ... or not to desire to be freed from fear" (TPT II. 296, emphasis added). The sovereign cannot compel conviction of any kind – hate, love, desire, and ambivalence – with the threat of violence, and so he should not bother trying to do so. Attempts to compel conviction are ultimately self-defeating, amounting to a practical – rather than principled – argument against persecution.

Yet Spinoza does not merely defend the freedom of judgment but suggests that this liberty extends to – even entails – the outward freedom of speech; after all, an individual should be allowed to freely "think, and judge, and *consequently also speak*," implying that the sovereign is powerless to control not merely judgment but also expression (TPT II. 346, emphasis added).[19] The significance of the language of "consequently" here cannot be overstated, as it suggests that Spinoza's defense of the freedom of judgment necessitates free speech, an intertwined relationship between two freedoms that are often viewed as concomitant but not necessarily interdependent. Like Milton, Spinoza argues that the liberty of conscience implies an outward freedom of expression; dissenters can speak freely because they enjoy liberty of conscience. The conflation of freedom of judgment and free speech, however, fails to account for the interpretive tension between Spinoza's earlier demands for the hypocritical conformity of outward behavior and his striking defense of free speech at the end of the *Treatise*.

Despite his suggestion that outward speech cannot be effectively compelled by the state, Spinoza invites his reader to consider the striking counterfactual of compelled expression in Chapter XX. This relatively neglected passage on hypocritical conformity is so provocative that it is worth quoting in its entirety:

[19] Susan James notes that individuals are prone to expression even when silence would behoove them: "Although individuals often pride themselves on being able to conceal their thoughts, 'not even the wisest know how to be silent', and 'it is a common vice of men to entrust their plans to others, even if there is no need for secrecy'." James, *Spinoza on Philosophy, Religion, and Politics*, 309.

> But suppose this freedom could be suppressed, and men so kept
> in check that they didn't dare to mutter anything except what
> the supreme powers prescribe. This would surely never happen in
> such a way that they didn't even think anything except what the
> supreme powers wanted them to. So the necessary consequence
> would be that every day men would think one thing and say
> something else. The result? The good faith especially necessary in
> a Republic would be corrupted. Abominable flattery and treachery
> would be encouraged, as would deceptions and the corruption of
> all liberal studies (TPT II. 349).

In this wonderfully strange passage, Spinoza wonders whether speech
could be compelled so that men never "dar[ed] to utter anything
except what the supreme powers prescribe," inviting speculation on
the very possibility of a world with homogeneous speech (TPT II.
349). Rather than insist on the futility of coercion to secure uniform
speech, Spinoza considers an example of the exact opposite; in this
hypothetical, hypocritical world in which no one speaks out of line,
the conformity of speech does not indicate unity of inward persuasion, a sociological reality that we can glean further from his recognition of the inevitability of pluralism. After all, individuals are
prone to radically different experiences of the same facts, such that it
is implausible that their public agreement reveals actual consensus.
While individuals might defer to their sovereign outwardly, Spinoza
argues that this would "surely never happen in such a way that they
didn't even think anything except what the supreme powers wanted
them to" (TPT II. 349). Even in this imagined world in which speech
could be compelled by the state, the inward persuasion of the subject
remains heterodox and unmoved despite his outward acquiescence.

By stressing the dissonance between conforming speech and
dissenting judgment, Spinoza diagnoses the outcome of persecution
as hypocritical conformity. The "necessary consequence" of a sovereign who compels outward expression will be insincere acquiescence,
or as Spinoza describes it, "every day men would think one thing and
say something else" (TPT II. 349, emphasis added). This compulsion

IV HYPOCRISY, "GOOD FAITH," AND CONSCIENTIOUS SPEECH 83

effectively amounts to the daily practice of insincere expression, in which dissenters consistently profess to hold views that do not correspond to their inward persuasion. Uniformity of opinion is impossible, as "it can't happen that [all men] speak with one voice" (TPT II. 346). In this imagined example, unity does not indicate cohesion but conformity. Even if it seems like persecution garners religious cohesion, Spinoza argues that it does not, in practice, secure real uniformity. In a powerful plea for *conscientious speech*, Spinoza wonders, "what greater evil can be imagined for the Republic than that honest men should be exiled as wicked because they hold different opinions and don't know how to pretend to be what they're not?" (TPT II. 350). For Spinoza, hypocritical conformity is too socially corrosive, making it difficult for individuals to trust others and punishing those who cannot feign outward obedience.

While the sovereign could force dissenters into religious uniformity, Spinoza warns that the inevitable implication of this coercion – hypocritical conformity – threatens freedom by undermining trust. Spinoza insists that hypocritical speech, or the outward expression of insincerely held views, erodes social relationships by breaking down the cultivation of trust among citizens. The immediate result of the ubiquitous practice of hypocrisy, he suggests, is that the "good faith especially necessary in a Republic would be corrupted" (TPT II. 349). The toleration of dissent means, in practice, that individuals cannot reasonably expect that others' outward confession is an accurate, conscientious reflection of their inward selves. Individuals learn to expect that others might perform a false misrepresentation of their convictions as compelled by the state. Rather than speak authentically, individuals might engage in outward conformity, inciting "abominable flattery and treachery," as well as "deceptions and corruption" (TPT II. 349). In a world characterized by hypocritical conformity, many individuals are forced to lie about their conscience, and this reality inevitably incites suspicion. Who is genuinely genuflecting? Who is dissimulating? In a state that demands hypocritical conformity, perception becomes suspect.

Several passages later in Chapter XX, Spinoza reaffirms this view that the intolerance of *conscientious speech* undermines trust: "Liberal studies and trust are corrupted, flatterers and traitors are encouraged, and the opponents [of liberal studies and trust] exult" (TPT II. 353). In a piercing critique of hypocritical conformity, Spinoza adds that "no one can fail to see that all these things are completely contrary to the well-being of the Republic," highlighting the significant threat of hypocrisy to the free republic (TPT II. 353). The repetitive language of "corruption" in this account stresses the corrosive consequences of hypocrisy on collaboration and cooperation. Even if individuals are not deceiving others, those around them remain suspicious. On this account, Spinoza does not merely defend *conscientious speech* by suggesting that the sovereign cannot coerce speech – he certainly can, even if their conformity will be insincere – but by arguing that hypocritical conformity undermines civic trust.

For Spinoza, the importance of trust can hardly be underestimated. In this counterfactual, Spinoza insists that "good faith" is "necessary" for a thriving, free republic (TPT II. 349). This diagnosis of the corrosive effects of compelled speech, moreover, parallels Spinoza's earlier account of the importance of trust in the *Treatise*: "With the utmost *good faith*, everyone would stand by their contracts completely, out of desire for this supreme good, the preservation of the Republic" (TPT II. 286, emphasis added). There, Spinoza associates "good faith" not only with honoring one's pledge in the form of a contract but with the very safeguarding of the republic. Again, Spinoza reiterates his view that trust is essential to the "chief protection of the Republic," suggesting that "good faith" underlies a stable and free republic (TPT II. 286). It is not surprising, then, given the centrality of trust to the very stability and cohesion of a republic that Spinoza places such a significant emphasis on sincerity in his defense of free speech and focuses specifically on potential threats to social trust. Individuals must be able to express their conscience freely so that others can assess their allegiances and alliances with confidence.

IV HYPOCRISY, "GOOD FAITH," AND CONSCIENTIOUS SPEECH 85

Spinoza's emphasis on trust differs, quite tellingly, from John Locke's concern with trust. John Dunn argues that, for Locke, human behavior "depends directly and profoundly on how far [individuals] can and should trust and rely upon one another."[20] Teresa Bejan also stresses the importance of *fides*, or "man's capacity to make and keep promises," in Lockean toleration.[21] Catholics and atheists were excluded from the scope of toleration precisely because they could not be expected to honor their "Promises, Covenants, and Oaths" without the threat of an "all-knowing God prepared to punish offenders."[22] Locke's concern with trust is grounded on a recognition that those without a commitment to divine retribution have no incentive to keep their word. Spinoza, however, is not concerned with whether a certain religious sect is more prone to breaking their promises but rather with the way that hypocritical conformity erodes social capital. For Locke, Protestants should not trust Catholics because they were not properly incentivized by divine retribution to honor their obligations to others. The issue at hand is not whether a dissenter's outward behavior is an authentic representation of the inward conscience, but how their beliefs make them more likely to deceive. For Spinoza, hypocritical conformity erodes the very possibility of trust itself by ensuring that one's outward expression is not a sincere reflection of one's inward persuasion, triggering mistrust and skepticism. The practice of hypocritical conformity in early modernity was so drastic that "concern[s] about wolves wearing sheep's clothing was a constant ingredient of the religious culture."[23] Trust is premised, Spinoza acknowledges, on a relative harmony between one's inward conscience and his outward expression, and hypocritical speech fundamentally disturbs this alignment.

---

[20] John Dunn, "The Concept of Trust in the Politics of John Locke," in *Philosophy in History: Essays on the Historiography of Philosophy*, eds. Richard Rorty, Jerome Schneewind, and Quentin Skinner (Cambridge: Cambridge University Press, 1984), 279.

[21] Bejan, *Mere Civility*, 136.

[22] Ibid.

[23] Walsham, *Charitable Hatred*, 161.

86 BARUCH SPINOZA AND CONSCIENTIOUS SPEECH

The very possibility of trust, on Spinoza's account, is premised on the toleration of *conscientious speech*, or in the negative, the absence of compelled speech. Spinoza returns to the relationship among hypocrisy, "good faith," and *conscientious speech* several passages later at the end of Chapter XX, reaffirming the corrosive repercussions of hypocritical speech:

> So, if *good faith, not flattering lip service ... is to be valued,* if the supreme powers are to retain their sovereignty as fully as possible, and not be compelled to yield to the rebellious, freedom of judgment must be granted. Men must be so governed that they can *openly hold different and contrary opinions,* and still live in harmony. There can be no doubt that this way of governing is best, and has the least disadvantages, since it's the one most compatible with men's nature (TPT II. 351, emphasis added).

This further appeal to "good faith" underlines the importance of trust in the republic, as it allows the sovereign "to retain their sovereignty as fully as possible" (TPT II. 351). To assure that citizens of a republic can trust that the words of others represent their convictions, they must be allowed to "openly hold different and contrary opinions" (TPT II. 351). In particular, Spinoza highlights two qualities of *conscientious speech* – its publicity and plurality. First, this speech must be "openly held," suggesting that individuals must be allowed to freely express their point of view without pressure or intimidation by the state. Second, dissenters must be free to express "different and contrary opinions," reaffirming the sociological realities of the deep differences among individuals. Rather than stress that citizens must be allowed to express dissenting views because the state cannot effectively coerce speech, Spinoza reaffirms his earlier endorsement of the corrupting consequences of hypocritical speech, offering his strongest warning against refusals to tolerate *conscientious speech*: "no doubt that this way of governing is best" (TPT II. 351).

This account of the potential threats to be thwarted by Spinoza's refutation of hypocritical expression aligns with his broader account

IV HYPOCRISY, "GOOD FAITH," AND CONSCIENTIOUS SPEECH 87

of the thesis of the *Treatise*. In the preface, Spinoza begins by suggesting that one of the central goals of his project is to show not only that the freedom of judgment and speech "[can] be granted without harm to the peace of the republic," but also that it *"cannot be taken away* without great danger to the peace and great harm to the whole Republic" (TPT II. 74, emphasis added). In the concluding passages of the *Treatise*, Spinoza returns to this central thesis, insisting again "not only that this freedom can be granted," but that it *"must* be granted, if we are to preserve" the republic, suggesting that any attempt to deny *conscientious speech* endangers the republic (TPT II. 353, emphasis added). This specific attention to "good faith" and hypocrisy underlies Spinoza's argument that refusals to protect speech are not only unproblematic but may even be perilous, threatening the very republic that they claim to be protecting.

Spinoza's account of *conscientious speech* raises questions about the consequences of dissent, especially in terms of the distinction between speech and behavior. He differentiates speech and behavior, suggesting that dissenters can speak publicly against the law but cannot violate it, even if it conflicts with their conscience. *Conscientious speech* might be too incendiary to the republic, requiring absolute hypocritical conformity to secure peace and stability, but insincere speech poses a greater threat to that very stability. Spinoza is careful, however, to delineate the limits of outward dissent. In particular, he defends *conscientious speech* as long as the dissenter "in the meantime does nothing contrary to what that law prescribes" (TPT II. 347). The dissenter, so excellent that Spinoza calls him "one of [the republic's] best citizens," can freely object to the law but cannot break it (TPT II. 347). This may require that he conform outwardly to the law, "act[ing] contrary to what he judges—and openly says—is good," but that requirement of conformity does not extend to his speech, which remains free to object to the sovereign (TPT II. 347). Some degree of outward, albeit hypocritical, conformity is necessary in a republic to protect sovereignty, but hypocritical speech seems to go too far by dangerously cultivating a culture of mistrust.

The crucial role of sincerity in promoting collaboration and cooperation justifies the toleration of *conscientious speech*, even if it means some degree of outward heterodoxy in practice.

Skeptics might worry that *conscientious speech* creates other problems that Spinoza does not fully appreciate, protecting even hateful or seditious forms of speech, which would surely undermine the fabric of civil society. Perhaps Spinoza does not understand the Hobbesian insight into the contentiousness of mere disagreement. But Spinoza does not suggest that speech does not do real harm. Speech, like conduct, can be quite harmful. As Susan James argues, Spinoza understood that "we do things with words, and some of the things we do with them are dangerous."[24] Yet he argues that *conscientious speech* must be tolerated nonetheless to avoid the danger of mistrust.

Despite Spinoza's concern with the disorder of difference, he does not suggest that all *conscientious speech* is tolerable. On his account, speech can be critical of political authority, for example, without being subject to restriction only if it is not paired with outward disobedience. Individuals should be allowed to speak whatever they want, "provided he takes no license from that to introduce anything into the Republic as a right, or *to do anything contrary to the accepted laws*" (TPT II. 353, emphasis added). For Spinoza, intolerable speech attempts to "nullify the law, seditiously," making the dissenter a "troublemaker and a rebel" rather than a critic (TPT II. 347). Here, very little consideration is given to the conscientious objection itself; what is at stake is whether the speech undermines the state.

There is a difference, Spinoza argues, between criticizing the state and subverting the authority of the state by obeying conscience as an alternative sovereign. An individual may fairly criticize a law, suggesting that it is "contrary to sound reason," as long as he obeys the law despite his disapproval. While he is allowed to "submit[t] his opinion to the judgment of the supreme power," with the goal

---

[24] James, *Spinoza on Philosophy, Religion, and Politics*, 311.

of changing the law, he must not act "contrary to what that law prescribes" despite the dictates of his conscience (TPT II. 347). An individual can be critical of a law, sharing that critique with the sovereign
even with the hopes of changing the law, but he must nonetheless
respect the law in his actions. Spinoza does suggest that some opinions are explicitly seditious by motivating certain acts. For example,
he mentions the opinion that one's sovereign is not "master," or that
individuals do not need to "keep his promises," or that "each person
ought to live according to his own decision," because these views
motivate individuals to partake in actions that undermine the state.
Yet these seditious opinions are seditious because they motivate
disobedience (TPT II. 347). As Susan James aptly notes, individuals
"should be free to express their opinions ... as long as their discourse
does not challenge the sovereign's right by violating the law."[25] This
dissenter respects but engages with the law, making them the "best
citizens" in a free republic (TPT II. 347). Spinoza's defense of *conscientious speech* does not hinge on the assumption that speech is
less harmful than action – indeed, Spinoza seems keenly aware that
speech can be extremely dangerous – but on the dangers of compelled
expression.

V CONCLUSION

By defending the freedom of *conscientious speech*, Spinoza urges
us to consider the socially corrosive repercussions of hypocritical
conformity and religious persecution beyond the encroachment on
the dissenter forced to conform. *Conscientious speech* suggests that
individuals must be free to speak in accordance with the dictates of
conscience to ensure civic trust. The violation of conscience thwarts
political collaboration and cooperation by breeding opacity and distrust among individuals. For Spinoza, individuals must be able to
trust that their outward behavior is an accurate representation of
their inward persuasion. Hypocritical conformity undermines civic

[25] Ibid., 312.

trust since individuals cannot ever fully trust if one's outward behavior is not merely a demonstration of obedience and conformity to the state. While Spinoza stresses the importance of sincere expression, he insists on hypocritical conformity in outward behavior. Politics cannot withstand the threat that liberty of conscience poses to political stability, urging dissenters to refuse to comply with the state's decrees. While liberty of conscience does not imply a license to "do anything," the state must allow individuals to express themselves in accordance with the dictates of their conscience to cultivate good faith among members of civil society.

Baruch Spinoza hopes that *conscientious speech* will secure freedom without undermining sovereignty, but free expression might not be enough to ensure "good faith" in a civil society. The promise of *conscientious speech* would hardly appease Pierre Bayle, another early modern refugee forced to flee his country due to religious persecution. Like Spinoza, Bayle is concerned with the psychological ramifications of hypocritical conformity, yet he focuses more on its effects on the mental well-being of the dissenter rather than the effects on society overall. Bayle's account of *tormented conscience* suggests that hypocritical conformity inflicts a meaningful psychological violation on the dissenter forced to choose between exile, death, and conformity. This psychological violation is not only felt as burdensome by the dissenter but also emboldens religious fervor. Bayle poignantly echoes an intuition about persecution that features across his contemporaries in this book – violations of conscience exacerbate conscience rather than tame it. Hypocritical conformity, Bayle warns, emboldens conscience.

5 Pierre Bayle and Tormented Conscience

I BAYLE AND "HALF-TOLERATION" MEN

While Baruch Spinoza offers a more measured view of toleration that demands dissenters engage in some degree of hypocritical conformity to safeguard stability and sovereignty, Pierre Bayle defends a much more radically tolerant view of liberty of conscience. In *Philosophical Commentary*, Bayle moves beyond a limited plea for the toleration of conscientious Protestant dissenters to a more inclusive view of toleration that extends to Jews, Muslims, and even atheists (although not Catholics). Indeed, Bayle argues that "Christian Princes cannot in justice expel the Mahometans out of Towns taken from the Turk, nor hinder their having Mosks, or assembling in their own House," suggesting a robust view of toleration and liberty of conscience that protects many forms of religious expression and worship.[1] Bayle's striking defense of the toleration of such a wide range of religious sects is a marked difference between him and many of his early modern contemporaries, or as Bayle condescendingly calls them, "half-toleration men." Many early modern figures, Bayle insists, fail to appreciate that all religious sects – not just one – should be tolerated.

Bayle's condemnation of religious persecution and hypocritical conformity is hardly an intellectual exercise. Bayle was forced to flee his homeland for the Dutch Republic as the Edict of Nantes – a law granting unprecedented rights to Calvinist Huguenots in Catholic France – was growing more tenuous. Bayle's brother, an ordained

---

[1] Pierre Bayle, *A Philosophical Commentary on These Words of the Gospel, Luke 14.23, "Compel Them to Come in, That My House May Be Full,"* ed. John Kilcullen and Chandran Kukathas (Indianapolis: Liberty Fund, 2005), 213. Hereafter cited in parenthetical citations as PC with page number.

92 PIERRE BAYLE AND TORMENTED CONSCIENCE

Calvinist minister, was imprisoned and would die in prison for his heterodox ministry. Despite his immediate experience with exile and imprisonment, Bayle concedes that many dissenters practice dissimulation to survive persecutory conditions. Of course, dissenters could flee their repressive homelands, as Bayle had done, or they could martyr themselves in death, but Bayle recognizes that most dissenters engage in hypocritical conformity. While critics of enforced conformity condemn dissimulation as a "despicable and damnable act of apostasy," Bayle acknowledges the ubiquity of the practice to "defus[e] suspicion and deflec[t] persecution."[2] The practice of hypocritical conformity shaped "everyday life in early modern Europe," from attendance at mandatory religious services to the omission of certain phrasing or bodily comportment. For example, dissenters would equivocate their compliance by reciting compulsory prayers in a muddled voice or refusing to remove their hats during a mandatory religious service.[3] Many dissenters responded "pragmatically and prudently to persecution," struggling to evade violence without violating their conscience.[4] Unlike Spinoza, who concedes that some degree of hypocritical conformity is necessary, Bayle stresses the dangers of this widespread compliance, reasonable given the immense threat of persecution but damaging nonetheless.

Many commentators trace Bayle's striking defense of the toleration of such a wide range of religious sects to his skepticism. Richard Popkin, the influential historian of skepticism, argues that the impossibility of certain divine knowledge assessed through reason, for the Pyrrhonian Bayle, undermines early modern justifications of persecution.[5] Given that we cannot "know or prove, through reason, the truth or falsity of any religion or the legitimacy or illegitimacy of any beliefs," it follows that the state must tolerate

---

[2] Walsham, *Charitable Hatred*, 196, 207.

[3] Hadfield, *Lying in Early Modern English Culture*, 20.

[4] Walsham, *Charitable Hatred*, 161.

[5] Richard Popkin, *The History of Scepticism: From Savanarola to Bayle, Expanded Edition* (Oxford: Oxford University Press, 2003), 283–302.

I BAYLE AND "HALF-TOLERATION" MEN 93

all religions, even those it views as profane, heretical, and erroneous.[6] Jonathan Israel stresses that "no philosopher uses skeptical
arguments more than Bayle," emphasizing that his skepticism is
grounded on "undercut[ting] grounds for belief."[7] Rainer Forst also
emphasizes skepticism in his account of Bayle's defense of a proto-
rationalist "reciprocity" view of toleration, suggesting that "any
argument for a general duty of mutual toleration has to rest on normative grounds accessible to and valid to believers of quite different
faiths (or of no faith)."[8] And finally, Chandran Kukathas argues that
"at the heart of [Bayle's] argument was the claim that the advocates
of compulsion were mistaken in asserting that they were justified in
enforcing conformity on the grounds of possession of the truth."[9] For
many influential commentators of early modern political thought
and toleration, Bayle defends toleration by arguing that the state cannot attest to the truth of its religion.

This scholarly preoccupation with Bayle's skepticism accounts
well for Bayle's more inclusive view of toleration. Given that there is
"no way to tel[l] an erring conscience from a nonerring one," defenders of Augustinian coercion cannot insist that they are justified in
compelling dissenters to the one "true" religion (PC 89). While "each
Sect looks on itself as the only true Religion, or at least much the
truest," allowing them to claim they do "great service to Truth" by
attempting to compel others to their religion, Bayle argues that it
is impossible to assess which religious tradition is the "true" one
(PC 89). By situating Bayle in a broader intellectual tradition that

---

[6] Ibid., 297.

[7] Jonathan Israel, *Enlightenment Contested: Philosophy, Modernity, and the
Emancipation of Man, 1670–1752* (Oxford: Oxford University Press, 2006), 267.

[8] Rainer Forst, "Pierre Bayle's Reflexive Theory of Toleration," in *Toleration and Its
Limits*, eds. Melissa Williams and Jeremy Waldron (New York: New York University
Press, 2008), 78; Rainer Forst, "Religion, Reason, and Toleration: Bayle, Kant—And
Us," in *Religion and Liberal Political Philosophy*, eds. Cécile Laborde and Aurelia
Bardon (Oxford: Oxford University Press, 2017), 249–261.

[9] Chandran Kukathas, "Toleration without Limits: A Reconstruction and Defense
of Pierre Bayle's Philosophical Commentary," in *Religion and Liberal Political
Philosophy*, 264.

recognizes the uncertainty of revealed truth, commentators show-case the powerful way that Bayle challenges the assertion of one "true" religion. Yet many proponents of persecution continue insisting on their "true" religion, and many dissenters are forced into conformity. To what extent does Bayle attend to the dangers inherent in this ubiquitous condition?

This chapter argues that Bayle attends to the psychological harm inflicted on the dissenter forced to conform. Bayle's *tormented conscience* suggests that infringements on conscience are felt as deep violations by the dissenter, an experience of mental torture akin to conventional forms of corporeal punishment that injure the physical body. Building on scholarly accounts that showcase the futility of coercion and skepticism as the central psychological justification underlying early modern toleration, I draw attention to Bayle's rich analysis of the broader psychological stakes in toleration and persecution. Not only does hypocritical conformity inflict mental torture on the dissenter forced to participate in a religious ceremony that violates his conscience, but persecution may even radicalize dissenters further. Demands for religious conformity do not convince dissenters of their error, as they are intended, but of their lack of zeal for their faith, rededicating them to their religion. By tracing Bayle's view of the mental effects of disingenuous outward confession and the unanticipated backlash it incites against the state in *Philosophical Commentary*, I recover the psychological strain inflicted on dissenters, forced to choose between fleeing their country, martyrdom, and their conscience.

Bayle's critique of religious persecution and its role in emboldening religiosity provides an alternative psychological intuition underlying early modern toleration and deepens our understanding of the mental dynamics at play in the politics of persecution. The central psychological intuition underlying early modern toleration is the futility of coercion to inspire genuine conversion. Commentators often frame Bayle's influential defense of toleration as grounded on a similar recognition that persecution merely pressures dissenters into false confessions. For example, Benjamin Kaplan describes Bayle as "extending the age-old dictum that faith could not be forced and that coercion only produced hypocrisy."[10] Yet Bayle points to alternative psychological intuitions motivating his critique of persecution that emphasizes the counterintuitive implications of persecution. By broadening our understanding of the psychological arguments in the early modern discourse on toleration and liberty of conscience, Bayle invites us to reflect on the counterintuitive implications of religious persecution, past and present.

By attending to the internal drama of the dissenter forced into conformity, Bayle urges us to consider the relationship between politics and the psychological well-being of the individuals in a political community. More repressive demands to obey the state, Bayle warns, may have counterintuitive consequences, emboldening dissenters to resist the state even more fervently. The dissonance between inward persuasion and outward behavior does not necessarily encourage the dissenter to change but may actually harden him in his views. Many advocates for conformity hope that exposure to certain ideas and practices and, in their more aggressive attempts, forced participation in these practices will slowly persuade dissenters of their heresy. However, Bayle warns that this response to religious sectarianism misrecognizes the enormous strain placed on the dissenter, forced to uncomfortably inhabit a false identity and perform disingenuous worship; moreover, this psychological torment is so unsettling that it actually encourages dissenters to cling more fervently to their beliefs. Bayle's view of *tormented conscience* invites us to reflect on the challenge of integrating a diverse community and the ways that attempts to engage nonconformists may backfire in unanticipated ways. Before examining Bayle's account of the psychological damage done by hypocritical conformity, it is helpful to begin with his account of defenses of persecution and his acknowledgment of the ubiquity of dissimulation in early modernity.

[10] Kaplan, *Divided by Faith*, 334.

II   HYPOCRITICAL CONFORMITY AND TORMENTED CONSCIENCE

Bayle's influential work on religious toleration is structured as an intellectual dialogue with his opponents. He engages with prevailing defenses of persecution in early modern discourse to "cut off the Convertists from all of their Starting-holes," especially the view that persecution is not harsh or reprehensible but a charitable effort to save dissenters from their damning heterodoxy (PC 140). Persecution is, its advocates insist, an act of Christian love and charity that brings dissenters closer to God and saves heretics from eternal damnation. Many early modern proponents of enforced conformity argue that religious persecution is a laudable tool to inspire conversion, a "bitter but efficacious medicine" intended to "cure and educate" heretics.[11] It was intended to work as a technique of persuasion aimed at "eliminat[ing] diversity of [religious] opinion by subjecting the populace to weekly doses of indoctrination in Protestant theology," thereby eroding religious heresy through exposure to the "true" religion.[12] Religious heterodoxy would "eventually wither out of existence," conformists insist, if dissenters were forced into consistent exposure to religious "truth."[13] Initially, proponents of conformity enlist legitimate means of persuasion, but they remain open to using violence as the "necessary" means to "force" dissenters "to deliver themselves from their Prejudices" (PC 79). Rather than call these measures "Persecution," they are treated as "Acts of Kindness, Equity, Justice, and right Reason" (PC 88). Measures of violence are, conformists argue, necessary to open dissenters to conversion. Bayle sets out to debunk the prevailing view that "Violence open[s] a Man's eyes to see his Heresy," suggesting rather that violence fails to accomplish this goal (PC 154). The consequences of persecution, Bayle argues, are "very far" from

---

[11] Walsham, *Charitable Hatred*, 2.
[12] Ibid., 60.
[13] Ibid.

II HYPOCRITICAL CONFORMITY AND TORMENTED CONSCIENCE 97

the desired conversion that persecutors hope to attain through measures of coercion (PC 140).

While Bayle argues that persecution does not achieve its intended goal of conversion, he concedes that it is very effective at encouraging outward behavior; even if it is futile, Bayle acknowledges that many dissenters conform to the state religion to avoid the very real threat of persecution. A "reasonable ... Man," Bayle acknowledges, is afraid of persecution, either of the "prospect of [his] Family ruin'd, exil'd, or encloister'd" or "of his own Person degraded and render'd incapable of all Honors and Preferments, and thrust into a loathsome Dungeon" (PC 139). Measures of persecution, or what he describes as "all the Crimes imaginable," among which he names "Murder, Robbery, Banishment, and Rapes," effectively compel outward conformity (PC 64). While violence or the threat of violence is "incapable ... of convincing the Judgment, or of imprinting in the Heart the Fear or the Love of God," it encourages dissenters to comply outwardly. Quite understandably, dissenters willingly engage in false professions and participate in disingenuous sacraments to escape the violent horrors that await them if they refuse. Given the very real risk of social ostracism, exile, or imprisonment, it is entirely sensible, Bayle argues, that dissenters conform to the state religion.

The severity of this violation hinges on the extent to which hypocritical conformity requires insincere outward behavior that violates conscience. Dissenters often engage in "some outward Signs void of all inward Sincerity," or even more strikingly, perform "Signs perhaps of an interior Disposition most opposite to that which [they] really are" when confronted with persecution (PC 78). Not only are dissenters willing to feign false acquiescence that they do not believe in, but they may be willing to act contrary to their conscience, an even more severe act of hypocrisy. The false performance of sacramental rights, what he describes as "Hypocrisy" and the "sacrilegious Profanation of Sacraments," harms the dissenter who violates his conscience to secure some degree of safety or standing in civil society (PC 64). Elsewhere, Bayle describes this conformity as "external Acts

98 PIERRE BAYLE AND TORMENTED CONSCIENCE

which are Hypocrisy and Imposture, or a downright Revolt against Conscience" (PC 64). Quickly thereafter, Bayle reiterates this language of revolution, suggesting that outward conformity is characterized by "Acts of Hypocrisy, and Falshood, or Impiety and Revolt against Conscience" (PC 77). Hypocritical conformity requires dissenters to commit a grave violation, acting directly at odds with their conscience.

While Bayle appreciates that persecution urges dissenters to engage in hypocritical conformity, he warns that this outward behavior inflicts psychological trauma on the compelled dissenter. His rich descriptions of revolt and violence stress the significant violation inflicted on dissenters, a kind of mental rather than corporeal injury. In his account of the religious dissenter forced to "adjure" outwardly "with [his] mouth," Bayle suggests that the conscientious dissenter "sink[s] under the Violence of Pain and Torment" (PC 58). In particular, Bayle recognizes that it is "very difficult ... for a body not to lye, when expos'd to the trial of the sharpest Sufferings," highlighting the severe mental burden of hypocritical conformity (PC 58). Elsewhere, Bayle criticizes proponents of conformity for taking advantage of this significant mental burden, reaffirming the psychological repercussions of hypocrisy:

> Our convertists will have Men threaten'd in the first place, and this condition annex'd, that they who *abjure shall be quit of all Persecution*, and stand fair for Rewards; and that their Threats may work the more efficaciously, the craftiest have a way of threatening such Deaths as are attended with slow and exquisite Torments, or depriving People of all means of flying, or subsisting at home. This constrains a world to betray the Lights of their Conscience, and *live afterwards under an Oppression of Spirit, which disorders, and at last drives 'em to despair*. What can be more cruel? (PC 182, emphasis added).

Defenders of conformity ask dissenters to choose between "abjur[ing]" outwardly or facing violent death, or as Bayle describes it, "slow and

II HYPOCRITICAL CONFORMITY AND TORMENTED CONSCIENCE 99

exquisite Torments" (PC 182). Again, it seems quite reasonable that dissenters engage in acts of "imposture" to avoid physical torture (PC 182). And yet Bayle warns of the unanticipated aftermath of this feigned conformity, "an oppression of Spirit, which disorders and at last drives 'em to despair" (PC 182). The severe and deep anguish provoked by conformity is hardly benign but is its own form of torture similar to more conventionally violent forms of persecution. Bayle reaffirms the severity of this psychological torment, describing it as living perpetually "in Anxiety and Remorse" (PC 182). In the provocative and blunt final line of the passage, Bayle invites his reader to speculate on this violation: "What could be more cruel?" (PC 182). This invocation of cruelty points toward the conflation of physical and mental torture, both experienced viscerally by the dissenter. The recurring language of torment and suffering throughout Bayle's examination of hypocritical conformity highlights the psychological distress experienced by the compelled believer, forced to choose between persecution and insincere profession, a continuous source of anguish even after the difficult decision has been made. Bayle does not merely defend toleration by suggesting that persecution presumes an impossible understanding of religious truth, but champions toleration as a way to end the psychological torture inherent in feigned conformity.

Bayle's treatment of heresy further reveals his concern with hypocritical conformity and *tormented conscience*. Since heretics are already "damn'd," there is no issue with forcing them to engage in hypocritical conformity (PC 540). Yet Bayle suggests that these proponents of persecution exacerbate the sin of the heretic. Conformists are not satisfied with allowing the heretic to "rest in his first sin," the very heresy itself, but are determined to aggravate their sin by adding the additional crime of "Hypocrisy ... a Sin against Conscience" to their iniquity (PC 540). The additional sin of hypocritical conformity, however, is not merely inconsequential but adds the burden of an "insupportable degree of Hell Torments," far more severe "than simple Heresy coul'd have merited" (PC 540). Here, Bayle invokes the language of "torment" to describe the additional burden inflicted on heretics; the language of "insupportable," moreover, emphasizes that this burden is deeply oppressive and overwhelming, verging on being insufferable.

The consequences of this psychological trauma can be severe, Bayle warns. Elsewhere, Bayle describes persecution as the "forcing" of "conscience" with "the most violent Temptations into Acts of Hypocrisy and deadly remorse," associating conformity with deep regret and guilt (PC 194). The qualifier of "deadly," moreover, implies the gravity of the burden of this remorse, so severe that it can be experienced as a kind of death. This gesture toward death is not merely intended to be hyperbolic but evokes practices of self-harm associated with early modern dissimulation. Dissenters experienced "very real distress" when forced to navigate the precarious position between the repressive demands of the sovereign and their consciences.[14] Indeed, some conformists suffered so greatly after their "agonizing" and "torment[ing]" acquiescence that they turned to suicide. They embraced death, "readily giv[ing] into the noose," as they were "overcome by the Extremity of Pain" following their compliance (PC 58).[15] The widespread demand for hypocritical conformity resulted in self-harm among dissenters.

Recent revisionist historiography supports Bayle's intuition that hypocritical conformity was deeply felt by dissenters and viewed by its perpetrators as a significant violation. Alexandra Walsham highlights that "oaths of allegiance and supremacy," were "devised as ... mechanisms for dividing true-hearted subjects from traitors," based on what conformists took to be their severe psychological consequences.[16] Demands for mandatory sacramental rights and oaths of allegiance were not merely attempts to secure "holy" uniformity but

---

[14] Ibid., 197.

[15] Ibid., 197–198. For example, Walsham offers the powerful example of a "Church Papist," a conforming Catholic who tried to drown himself after reciting the common prayer of the Church of England.

[16] Walsham, "Ordeals of Conscience," 36.

were intended to expose heresy. Hypocritical conformity was viewed as imposing an immense psychological tax on dissenters such that they would disclose themselves, effectively operating as "mechanical lie-detectors to discover who hid their false opinions behind the cloak of conformity."[17] Proponents of persecution, Bayle argues, recognize the severe impact of measures of coercion, noting that the very "Design of these Torments was only to make 'em confess themselves" (PC 58). While many proponents of persecution insist that they were ambivalent about inward persuasion, as long as conformity was practiced outwardly, Bayle recognizes that conformists were relying on the psychological trauma of hypocritical conformity to pressure dissenters to expose themselves as such.

This account of the psychological damage of hypocritical conformity raises the broader question of the political implications of *tormented conscience*. Of course, we might read Bayle's concern with the mental repercussions of religious persecution on the dissenter sincerely; he may have been genuinely concerned with the tortured dissenter forced into the "imposture" of hypocritical conformity. But we might also consider Bayle's concern with *tormented conscience* in light of his broader suggestion that persecution, rather than toleration, incites political upheaval. Elsewhere in the *Philosophical Commentary*, Bayle suggests that attempts to secure "holy uniformity" incite political conflict; we only need to consult history to see that "all the Disturbances attending Innovations in Religion, proceed from People's pursuing the first Innovators with Fire and Sword, and refusing 'em a Liberty of Conscience" (PC 201). This somber assessment of the potential consequences of persecution resonates with Hobbes's treatment of compulsion, in which he argues that attempts to coerce inward conviction exacerbate political conflict by provoking zealous dissenters. Religious dissenters might not merely suffer needlessly at the hands of hypocritical conformity but also react aggressively out of resentment against the enforcers of

[17] Ibid.

PIERRE BAYLE AND TORMENTED CONSCIENCE

their mental torture. In this way, Bayle's account of *tormented conscience* broadens up to a social critique of hypocritical conformity, parallel to Spinoza's concern that hypocritical conformity corrodes one's ability to assess if his neighbor is sincere or an imposter.

Like Spinoza, who recognizes the inevitability of the pluralism of "opinions" and the "variability" of "judgments" among individuals, Bayle views religious difference as inevitable. One might expect those who view difference as divisive to defend any attempt to ensure religious uniformity. While Bayle acknowledges that "Unity and Agreement," especially "Agreement among Christians in the Profession of one and the same Faith," would be an "invaluable Blessing," uniformity is not possible in the first place (PC 208). Bayle acknowledges that unity would be desirable, but he suggests that the human condition is doomed to be characterized by pluralism, recognizing that a "difference in Opinions seems to be Man's inseparable Infelicity" (PC 208). Difference is inevitable, reframing the debate from the most effective strategy to eliminate difference to a conversation on peaceful coexistence. Given the inevitability of diversity, toleration is a "smaller Evil, and less shameful to Christianity," than the severe measures of persecution, such as "Massacres, Gibbets, Dragooning, and all the bloody Executions," which the "Church of *Rome* has continually endeavor'd to maintain unity, without being able to encompass it" (PC 140; emphasis in original). Pluralism is unavoidable, even if unity would be preferred, and the violence used to overcome it will be considerably detrimental to our political communities.

Moreover, as is evident from the history of the Catholic Church, persecution has hardly been successful. Difference divides communities, Bayle acknowledges, but it is attempts to compel uniformity that pose the most critical threat to social stability. For Bayle, attempts to compel conscience with a sword incite ceaseless conflict. Unlike Hobbes, who is notoriously worried about the divisive consequences of religious sectarianism, Bayle argues that it is the very *persecution* of these differences that breeds the kind of civil disorder that so concerned Hobbes. It is not difference itself that incites conflict; attempts to *thwart* difference lead to the kind of violence that characterizes the Hobbesian state of nature. For Hobbes and many of his absolutist contemporaries, the "Multiplicity of Religions" places "Neighbor at variance with his Neighbor, Father against Son, Husbands against their Wives, and the Prince against his Subjects" (PC 199). Yet Bayle offers an alternative account of the source of division in society, suggesting that attempts to compel conformity breed civil disorder. We only need to consult history, Bayle suggests, to see that "all the Disturbances attending Innovations in Religion, proceed from People's pursuing the first Innovators with Fire and Sword, and refusing 'em a Liberty of Conscience" rather than "the new Sect's attempting, from an inconsiderable Zeal, to destroy the Religion establish'd" (PC 201). Attempts to compel conscience are far more divisive than conscience itself. Liberty of conscience is not necessarily divisive, but attempts to coerce conscience are volatile. Conflict does not arise from pluralism itself but from attempts to "exercise a cruel Tyranny" over dissenters and "force Conscience" (PC 200). In short, "all the Mischief arises not from Toleration, but from the want of it" (PC 200). He continues to stress this point: "Nothing therefore but Toleration can put a stop to all those Evils; nothing but a Spirit of Persecution can foment' em" (PC 201). Religious persecution and hypocritical conformity actually embolden religiosity by attempting to restrict it. Simply put, it is less contentious to allow dissenters to "serv[e] God according to the Light of their Consciences" rather than "murder and torment [them] by a thousand exquisite ways" (PC 63). Bayle echoes his account of *tormented conscience*, suggesting that it is a kind of torture akin to murder yet distinct from corporeal violence. Religious persecution inflicts a meaningful violation on dissenters, inciting more political upheaval than that inherent in religious sectarianism. For Spinoza and Bayle, the appropriate response to the realities of religious difference is to allow individuals to pursue their own views, as these differences only become salient politically when individuals try to compel others into submission.

III CONFORMITY AND ZEALOTRY

Bayle's *tormented conscience* suggests that infringements on conscience can be felt as deep violations by dissenters, forced to conform and live with the distressing consequences of hypocritical conformity long after the act of "imposture." Religious persecution inflicts meaningful psychological violations on dissenters who inhabit this dissonance between inward conscience and outward behavior. Not only does persecution fail to accomplish the very goal that its proponents of persecution claim to pursue, but it also inspires dissenters to cling to their heterodox religion more fiercely. Like Hobbes who stresses the counterintuitive effects of persecution which "exasperate" dissenters, Bayle foregrounds the inevitable yet surprising outcome of persecution – resentment of the state and reinvigorated religious fanaticism.

Despite the significant threat to the mental and physical security of the religious dissenter, punishments "very rarely change Mens Opinions about the Worship of God" (PC 304). They actually have the opposite effect of "mak[ing] [dissenters] more zealous in their own Religion" (PC 304). The false performance of a religious sacrament, for example, does not urge dissenters to consider the "Falseness of [their] Religion," but inspires them to ponder their "want of Zeal for it" (PC 304). The "Persecuted," Bayle insists, are "drawn into ... a wickeder ... Imposture by outwardly renouncing a Religion, which in their Souls they were more firmly persuaded of than ever" (PC 106). The hypocrisy of insincere outward professions exacerbates their "wicked" heresy even further, moving them to be more "firmly persuaded" of their religion (PC 106). Hypocritical conformity is not inconsequential but convinces dissenters of their religion more fervently than they had been previously.

Elsewhere, Bayle reiterates the counterintuitive implications of measures of coercion intended to convert the souls and hearts of the unorthodox, suggesting that a dissenter is "more confirm'd in his own [Religion] ... from the tyrannical methods [the state] employs against him" (PC 139). This invocation of "firmness" stresses the emboldening – rather than withering – of religious zeal. This potential for fervor is not unique to any specific religion but hinges on a psychological intuition about the aggravation of persecution. Catholics will "become more Popish than they were before," and Muslims will "grow more zealous and obstinate in Mahometism," if persecuted (PC 155). Hypocritical conformity, Bayle warns, has the precisely opposite effect of its intended goal.

Bayle offers up two examples of the counterintuitive effects of religious persecution. The former focuses on the state, and the latter foregrounds a religious leader. First, Bayle describes a hypothetical political state that closely resembles his homeland, France. He invites his reader to suppose that the state views Catholicism as the "true Church" and consider the "Consequences of Compulsion" (PC 155). What are the consequences of "threaten[ing] those who persis[t] in their Heresy with the roughest Treatment?" Bayle asks (PC 155). Dissenters, Bayle argues, "gr[ow] more zealous in their Religion than ever" (PC 154). Persecution does not ensure the religious uniformity of this imagined political society but radicalizes dissenters. This religious zeal manifests in austere measures of religious practice, such as "continual Fastings and extraordinary Humiliations," demonstrating their heightened religiosity (PC 154). Dissenters view persecution as a providential sign that they should commit themselves even more fiercely to their religion.

Second, Bayle offers up a corresponding example of a religious leader who compels dissenters into false worship. He elaborates on an example of a pastor who is "sincerely zealous for the Salvation of his Flock," even enlisting coercive measures to try to convince dissenters of his religion (PC 300). Yet Bayle reaffirms his warning that these kinds of measures of coercion do not invite dissenters in but ostracize them: "Men being much more apt to be embitter'd and confirm'd in their Opinions by harsh Treatment, than determin'd to change and forsake 'em" (PC 300). For Bayle, persecution does not deliver on its presumed goal of inspiring dissenters to abandon

106 PIERRE BAYLE AND TORMENTED CONSCIENCE

their heterodoxy and embrace the one true, saving religion; rather, it estranges them from the state and intensifies their attachment to their religion.

Early modern historians have recovered this emboldening effect, suggesting that dissenters experienced the repression of the state as a divine sign of the need for religious zeal. Alexandra Walsham stresses that the early modern "social experience of diaspora and displacement often helped to strengthen the religious commitment of those who undertook it," recognizing the significant impact of exile and ostracism on dissenters and refugees like Bayle.[18] Many measures of persecution "galvanized the faith" of religious dissenters.[19] Persecution does not convince dissenters of their heresy but "intensif[ied] and catalyz[ed] the conviction that one was a member of the predestinate elect."[20] For advocates of conformity, persecution is intended to convince dissenters that they are "afflicted [by] a false Religion" (PC 154). Yet persecution and the many "Evils" dissenters are forced to confront are attributed to their "want of Zeal for [their] Religion, to their Lukewarmness in its services" (PC 154). Persecution does not undermine religious heterodoxy but inspires dissenters to be even more fanatical in their religious practice and commit themselves more fully to religious rituals. Persecution implies this strange tension, which is both disturbing and energizing. Suffering is "at the same time immensely empowering," not necessarily demoralizing dissenters but inspiring them to commit even more fiercely to their religion.[21] Bayle's *tormented conscience* suggests that meaningful violations of conscience may not only distress dissenters but may vex them so deeply that they respond with fanaticism.

---

[18] Walsham, *Charitable Hatred*, 186.
[19] Ibid.
[20] Ibid.
[21] Ibid., 212.

IV CONCLUSION

By showcasing the profound psychological implications of religious persecution, Bayle invites us to reflect on the cognitive harm done by hypocritical conformity. To what extent can dissenters conform without violating their conscience? Or does hypocritical conformity invade their conscience so intensely that it antagonizes them? Bayle's *tormented conscience* suggests that hypocritical conformity does not merely demand negligible compliance with the state but inflicts meaningful psychological distress on the dissenter and emboldens him further. Early modern theories of toleration emphasize the futility of coercion to shape inward persuasion, but Bayle warns that attempts to convince others of their misjudgments may also backfire, an appeal that remains powerful even today.

6 The Politics of Conscience

I LIBERTY OF CONSCIENCE AND EARLY MODERNITY

These early modern critiques of hypocritical conformity might seem irrelevant given recent invocations of liberty of conscience in contemporary American politics. As Saba Mahmood declares in her measured account of political equality and minority rights, "conscience has become the defining feature of religious liberty."[1] Recent efforts in political theory to grapple with the implications of this longstanding freedom are not merely superficial dismissals of an outdated concept but reveal a deeper anxiety that liberty of conscience cannot safeguard the rich religious pluralism that characterizes our modern world. By privileging majoritarian religions over minoritarian ones, liberty of conscience undermines the very freedom that it promises to protect in the first place. Liberty of conscience is, simply put, "bound with [an] inadequate, ethnocentric, and Christian understanding of what religion is."[2] By privileging religious conviction over other forms of religious expression, worship, or community, liberty of conscience is incompatible with many religions as they are lived and practiced today. For these commentators, liberty of conscience should be reconfigured, reimagined, or abandoned for a more inclusive, egalitarian concept without such significant historical and intellectual baggage. Other commentators stress the inequitable application of liberty of conscience in practice. For example, liberty of conscience is often narrowly afforded to Christians, Asma Uddin argues, while Muslims are not afforded the same protections,

[1] Mahmood, *Religious Difference in a Secular Age: A Minority Report* (Princeton: Princeton University Press, 2015), 49, fn. 70.
[2] Ibid., 4.

urging a more equitable invocation of liberty of conscience.[3] And finally, there is a growing suspicion that liberty of conscience is merely a smokescreen for exclusion and prejudice. While liberty of conscience has historically been safeguarded in American politics, it is increasingly invoked to further hate and oppression rather than protect minoritarian religions. This growing ambivalence, at best, and hostility, at worst, toward liberty of conscience urged my reconsideration of this longstanding freedom and its intellectual origins in this book.

These theoretical attempts to challenge, or at the very least complicate, our longstanding commitment to liberty of conscience are hardly unwarranted. Indeed, American politics requires some degree of compliance with democratic laws and norms for politics to function. In asking to be exempt from democratic laws that conflict with their conscience, dissenters undermine the rule of law. Influential critics of liberty of conscience have offered a useful corrective to the received view of liberty of conscience, which overlooks its potential abuses and unequal applications. However, they seem to have pushed too far in the other direction, overstating a stylized story about early modern toleration and the implications of liberty of conscience. Simply put, why should we protect liberty of conscience in the first place? And what are the potential disadvantages of limiting it?

These early modern defenses of liberty of conscience suggest that influential critics of the concept overlook the political, social, and psychological threats that hypocritical conformity poses to political life. Milton, Hobbes, Spinoza, and Bayle's critiques of hypocritical conformity are theoretical attempts to diagnose and grapple with the disengagement, distrust, and distress inflicted by restrictions on liberty of conscience in early modern society. For these figures, it is not necessary to safeguard liberty of conscience because of

---

[3] Asma Uddin, *When Islam Is Not a Religion: Inside America's Fight for Religious Freedom* (New York: Pegasus Books, 2019).

the sanctity of conscience, but because there are real and meaningful consequences to politics characterized by conformity. These four figures point toward deeper and arguably more discerning anxieties about conformity and hypocrisy – the thwarting of the capacities of political citizenship, the improbability of acquiescence, the corrosion of social trust among members of a political community, and the significant psychological trauma inflicted on the dissenter. For these four figures, hypocritical conformity has underappreciated and pernicious implications worth considering in the delicate balancing act and complex tradeoffs inherent in protections – and refusals – of conscience.

Milton's *expressive conscience* urges us to consider liberty of conscience as part of a broader constellation of freedoms. Liberty of conscience, for Milton, implies expressive, outward, and public freedoms, since this experience of expression is the very process through which conscience is cultivated. Conscience, Milton argues, must be exercised, like a muscle that demands movement and training. Hypocritical conformity thwarts opportunities for individuals to exercise their conscience, thereby languishing this crucial capacity of political citizenship. By engaging in the false worship of hypocritical conformity, dissenters are made slavish and indiscriminate. Liberty of conscience, Milton argues, must be granted to all individuals in a political society, or citizens will not have the opportunity to cultivate the capacities of freedom. Freedom, for Milton, is not merely concerned with the conditions of freedom but also with the capacities of freedom.

Hobbes's *instilled conscience* suggests that dissenters will not willingly comply with laws that conflict with their conscience and envisions civic education as a solution to the intractable politics of conscience. Unlike his contemporaries, Hobbes focuses on a prior and arguably more crucial question at the center of the debate on liberty of conscience – what is the origin of conscience in the first place? Hobbes diagnoses appeals to conscience for what they really are – profound manifestations of competing political authorities. Yet

I   LIBERTY OF CONSCIENCE AND EARLY MODERNITY   III

the very solution to the problem of liberty of conscience itself lies in this fact. If contemporary invocations of conscience are reflective of dueling allegiances to competing sovereigns, then the sovereign must oversee the education of conscience. Civic education provides a promising path forward – mild enough to avoid inciting further zeal but effective enough to impede differences of conscience. For Hobbes, conscience is one of the most meaningful threats to social and political stability, and civic education is an equally powerful strategy to overcome this threat.

Spinoza's *conscientious speech* acknowledges the social dangers inherent in hypocritical conformity, specifically the impairing of civic trust. While widespread dissimulation might secure the pretense of religious uniformity, it undermines civic trust among members of a political community. In a world characterized by hypocritical conformity, individuals anticipate deceit and duplicity in their fellow citizens; they constantly question whether the outward behavior of others is sincere or coerced, and this constant doubt corrodes the necessary trust to sustain even the most basic level of political collaboration and coordination.[4] By stressing the precondition of authenticity in cultivating trust, Spinoza suggests that *conscientious speech* is not merely a problem to overcome in politics but also the necessary foundation for politics, a rather counterintuitive idea that justifies the protection of liberty of conscience.

And finally, Bayle's *tormented conscience* reflects on the psychological effects of hypocritical conformity on the conscientious dissenter. Political and social pressures to dissimulate, especially in ways that violate our conscience, are not insignificant, Bayle warns, but can be deeply destructive to an individual's mental well-being. The experience of conforming does not only corrode social relationships among citizens but also asks individuals to bifurcate their private self from their public one, resulting in the isolating and

---

[4] David Runciman, *Political Hypocrisy: The Mask of Power, from Hobbes to Orwell and Beyond, Revised Edition* (Princeton: Princeton University Press, 2018), 1.

112 THE POLITICS OF CONSCIENCE

psychologically taxing experience of suppressing the outward expression of one's true self. Hypocritical conformity is not merely a trivial demand that requires dissenters to engage in behaviors that they do not believe in with little consequence to their conscience, but a deeply felt violation that reverberates through the dissenter even long after the act of conformity is complete. Bayle's *tormented conscience* also urges us to consider the aggravation inspired by demands for hypocritical conformity, as dissenters will deepen their commitments to their conscience rather than absorb the laws and norms of the state. Conscience is not hindered by demands for hypocritical conformity but emboldened, urging us to reconsider how we approach zealous appeals to conscience. Together, these four figures urge us to broaden our understanding of the stakes surrounding the liberty of conscience and attend to the underappreciated implications of refusals to accommodate conscience. While hypocritical conformity might abate disagreement, promote social uniformity, and secure equality among citizens, Milton, Hobbes, Spinoza, and Bayle warn that it might also have unforeseen consequences worth considering, or at the very least, worth anticipating, in politics.

II THE POLITICS OF CONSCIENCE

In concluding, this book moves beyond early modernity and returns to the contemporary crisis of conscience afflicting American politics that urged my reconsideration of the intellectual origins of liberty of conscience in the first place. I focus on two less familiar cases concerning liberty of conscience in American politics, one about a florist who refuses to design floral arrangements for a same-sex wedding and another about a humanitarian aid worker who harbors undocumented migrants at the US–Mexico border. In turning from early modern debates on toleration and liberty of conscience to these contemporary controversies, I hope to accomplish three goals. First, I aim to broaden our understanding of the kinds of controversies that involve liberty of conscience in American politics by exploring how one Christian faces psychological turmoil when refusing to participate in a same-sex wedding celebration and considering how a more progressive dissenter refuses to conform to immigration laws. These cases, especially the second one, challenge the now-familiar association of the politics of conscience with Christian evangelicals and remind us of the ways that conscience might enable us to pursue a more just and equitable world.

Second, I set out to glean insights from early modern defenses of liberty of conscience and critiques of hypocritical conformity for contemporary debates on religion and politics. This book aims to understand these early modern figures on their own terms – to understand their arguments as well as the context and constraints that shaped their political thought – but my engagement with them also provides us with an occasion to reflect on our political commitments. I do not mean to suggest that Milton and Hobbes offer us immediate answers to our contemporary controversies; they could not have anticipated the contours of contemporary politics and the many conflicts that plague us today. Yet these early modern figures, I suggest, broaden our understanding of the stakes of these controversies beyond the obvious and surely important concerns with the rule of law and equality. By engaging with these two specific case studies, I show how these figures sharpen our understanding of these controversies and challenge our intuitions about them. The question of how to grapple with contemporary invocations of conscience, as I suggested in the introduction, is a question we must answer for ourselves, but these figures enrich our thinking about this urgent question.

And finally, I reflect on the limits of thinking with these four early modern figures, acknowledging their enduring insights alongside their inevitable blind spots. While these figures deepen our understanding of the implications of the politics of conscience, they privilege certain concerns over others and fail to address other concerns that are crucial for us. These figures, I suggest, should guide our thinking by cautioning us of potential blind spots in our own political thought.

The theological, social, and political context of early modernity is, of course, dramatically distinct from our contemporary one.

114 THE POLITICS OF CONSCIENCE

Persecution is not pluralism, and contemporary controversies on liberty of conscience are wildly different from early modern ones. While early modern controversies on liberty of conscience were concerned with the false profession of religious persuasion to avoid penalty or punishment, contemporary controversies on liberty of conscience often focus on commercial exchanges or exemptions from generally applicable laws. Yet even contemporary American politics seems increasingly afflicted by pervasive threats to trust, authenticity, and accountability that recall the political, social, and psychological fracturing done by early modern practices of religious dissimulation. The extent to which conscience should be accommodated when it conflicts with democratic laws remains an urgent question today, especially given the polarization of the political and social landscape, as well as historic mistreatment of minoritarian religions in American politics. For Milton, Hobbes, Spinoza, and Bayle, the question of whether the state should protect liberty of conscience, as well as what protecting liberty of conscience actually meant in practice, was one of the central questions of their time. This question, while it has certainly morphed in shape, continues to dominate our contemporary moment; their thinking, as such, remains strangely relevant to us today, even if their historical context is distinct.

III   *ARLENE'S FLOWERS* AND THE PSYCHOLOGY OF CONSCIENCE

While *Masterpiece Cakeshop* has dominated conversations on religious freedom in American politics, *Arlene's Flowers* v. *State of Washington* arguably sheds more light on the political and psychological stakes of these conflicts between conscience and the equality and dignity of marginalized individuals. Like *Masterpiece Cakeshop*, *Arlene's Flowers* centers on a conscientious refusal to participate in a same-sex wedding, yet it raises distinct psychological questions about conscience due to the established client relationship between the owner of the florist, Baronelle Stutzman, and her client, Robert Ingersoll. This case involves a local florist in Washington

III ARLENE'S FLOWERS AND THE PSYCHOLOGY OF CONSCIENCE 115

state, Arlene's Flowers, owned and run by Stutzman. Stutzman has a longstanding client relationship with Ingersoll who regularly uses Arlene's Flowers for floral arrangements for holidays and celebrations. Stutzman and Ingersoll seem to have an amenable, even affable, client relationship. Stutzman describes "hitting it off from the beginning" with Ingersoll, highlighting their shared passion for floral artistry.[5] Stutzman describes Ingersoll as a "friend," and Ingersoll calls Arlene's Flowers his "favorite floral shop."[6] Stutzman and Ingersoll's relationship, at first blush, is an encouraging example of collaboration in our deeply polarized society. Stutzman often arranges flowers for Ingersoll's same-sex partner, Curt Freed, for their anniversaries, despite her Baptist religious affiliation. Ingersoll enjoys working with Stutzman on floral designs, despite her more conservative social views and religious background. Their client relationship suggests that American citizens can not only coexist peacefully despite their dramatically distinct worldviews but can even collaborate productively.

This is, however, not the whole story. After *Obergefell* and the legalization of same-sex marriage, Ingersoll and Freed decided to get married. They began planning a large wedding celebration, and one of their first decisions during the planning process was to ask Stutzman, their florist, to design the flowers for their wedding. Stutzman refused Ingersoll's inquiry, citing her religious views about the union of marriage and her conscientious objection to same-sex marriage. While Stutzman had an established client relationship with Ingersoll, even designing him flowers to give his partner for their anniversaries, she felt conflicted about decorating a same-sex wedding. While Stutzman felt conflicted about contributing creatively to a same-sex wedding, she also felt conflicted about refusing Ingersoll,

---

[5] Barronelle Stutzman, "Why a Friend Is Suing Me: The Arlene's Flowers Story," *Seattle Times*, November 9, 2015, www.seattletimes.com/opinion/why-a-good-friend-is-suing-me-the-arlenes-flowers-story.

[6] Curt Freed and Robert Ingersoll, "Why We Sued Our Favorite Florist: Marriage Equality Must Be Truly Equal," *Seattle Times*, October 31, 2015, www.seattletimes.com/opinion/why-true-marriage-equality-matters-to-us.

her longstanding client and friend. Stutzman describes this exchange with Ingersoll as deeply challenging: "It was a painful thing to try to explain to someone I cared about – one of the hardest things I've ever done in my life."[7] Stutzman's description of the encounter suggests that she cares deeply about Ingersoll and that she does not take her refusal lightly. She appreciates that her refusal will hurt Ingersoll and Freed and acknowledges the dignitarian harm that will be done to the couple. While Stutzman does not want to hurt Ingersoll, she feels compelled to refuse his request. Stutzman's description of her experience of inner turmoil suggests that individuals cannot easily conform to the law if it conflicts with their conscience, experiencing enormous strain on their conscience.

This initial exchange ends relatively uneventfully, especially given the gravity of the situation. Stutzman reports that this conversation goes relatively well in the moment. She offers up a few alternative florists who might work with Ingersoll on his wedding. Ingersoll "assured" Stutzman that he "understood" her decision, and the two even "seemed to part as friends."[8] Yet Ingersoll was, understandably, deeply hurt by this refusal. Ingersoll and Freed are dissuaded from their original plans to celebrate their marriage in a large wedding celebration because of Stutzman's refusal and the unsettling uncertainty and insecurity that it invites: "Would other businesses turn us down for being gay?.... What if our ceremony became the target of anti-gay activists from other states?"[9] While Ingersoll does not express frustration in the initial exchange, it is clear that Stutzman's refusal inflicts significant distress on the couple.

Ingersoll and Freed sue Stutzman, and the case reaches the Washington Supreme Court. The Court determines that Stutzman could not refuse service to Ingersoll on the basis of his sexual orientation. The Court held that Stutzman's conscience does not exempt her from generally applicable laws, especially anti-discrimination

---

[7] Stutzman, "Why a Friend Is Suing Me."

[8] Ibid.

[9] Freed and Ingersoll, "Why We Sued Our Favorite Florist."

III ARLENE'S FLOWERS AND THE PSYCHOLOGY OF CONSCIENCE 117

laws intended to protect and promote equality among citizens. After *Masterpiece Cakeshop*, Stutzman appealed her case to the Supreme Court of the United States, which sent the case back to the Washington Supreme Court. The Washington Court determined that *Masterpiece* had no bearing on *Arlene's Flowers* because the state did not display animus toward Stutzman's religion as it had toward Jack Phillips's religion. In the case of the balancing act between Stutzman's conscience and Ingersoll's right to equality and dignity, the latter triumphs over conscience.

These four early modern figures urge us to resist overly-simplistic answers to contemporary debates, such as confining conscience to the inner sphere of the mind or endowing conscience with absolute authority – a kind of "trump card" that justifies any and all dissent. The politics of conscience requires a delicate balancing act between liberty of conscience and, at times, competing liberties and political commitments; these figures draw out shades of gray in an otherwise polarizing debate often cast in black and white. For example, Milton's *expressive conscience* invites us to consider ways to protect equality while also safeguarding liberty of conscience. For Milton, infringements on conscience should be minimized to the extent possible, inflicting the "least bruise on conscience." Stutzman's conscience should have been protected to the greatest extent possible, exempting her from anti-discrimination laws that infringe on her conscience. The Miltonic approach to these invocations of conscience might mean exempting these individuals from anti-discrimination laws and placing the burden on same-sex couples to seek out florists and bakers who do not have a conscientious conflict with same-sex marriage. Douglas Laycock defends a Miltonic approach to conscience by suggesting that same-sex couples should be granted the liberty to get married, but we need not ask "religious believers with deep moral objections" to be a part of celebrating these unions.[10] This, of course,

---

[10] Douglas Laycock, "Religious Liberty and the Culture Wars," *University of Illinois Law Review* 3 (2014): 839–880, 879.

overlooks the state's interest in promoting equality among democratic citizens and protecting the L.G.B.T.Q.I.A.+ community from dignitarian harms. In the balancing act between safeguarding conscience and promoting equality, Milton asks us to consider whether conscience could have prevailed to a greater degree.

It is important to acknowledge that these compromises are often costly or untenable. First, reasonable accommodations for florists like Stutzman who do not want to participate in same-sex wedding ceremonies present obvious challenges. While Stutzman offers up alternative florists to work with Ingersoll, this accommodation is more complicated in practice based on the geographic clustering of certain social and religious views. This regional issue is severe, for example, in debates on reproductive freedom and conscientious objections among medical professionals in Italy, in which many Catholic doctors refuse to perform abortions, effectively resulting in a de facto restriction on abortion across the country.[11] Even while recognizing that this delicate balance is not necessarily feasible in all situations, Milton urges us to strive toward compromises and look for possible paths forward to safeguard both conscience and other political goals and commitments. Second, the blind spots in Milton's political thought invite us to reflect on the blind spots in our thinking. To what extent are toleration and liberty of conscience extended to all religions in American politics today? In what ways are our attempts to promote toleration intolerant today? By defending the liberty of conscience of some dissenters while condemning the liberty of conscience of others, Milton reminds us that toleration is not necessarily extended equally to all, even if it is afforded to some.

While Milton advocates for the minimization of infringements on conscience, Hobbes considers whether invocations of liberty of conscience undermine civil stability and political authority. Contemporary invocations of conscience, commentators insist, are unprecedented, a deviation from this otherwise innocuous principle.

[11] Mancini and Rosenfeld, *The Conscience Wars*, 1–2.

Douglas NeJaime and Reva Siegel describe recent appeals to conscience as "complicity-based," suggesting that individuals are newly insistent that they should not have to be complicit in the sins of others, a more invasive view of an individual's conscientious scruples toward certain conduct.[12] Susanna Mancini and Michel Rosenfeld describe recent appeals to conscience as uniquely "interventionist and intrusive."[13] For these commentators, Stutzman is asking for far more than liberty of conscience. After all, Stutzman is free to believe in her own understanding of marriage, as well as live out that understanding of marriage in her own life. What she is asking for, commentators stress, is not only an exemption from a democratic law intended to protect equality among citizens but also to impose her conscience on the conduct of others. *Arlene's Flowers* is not about whether Stutzman can live out her conscientious view of marriage in her own life, but how she should be able to relate to others in her community through commercial exchanges. Commentators insist that invocations of conscience by individuals like Stutzman are newly contentious, far exceeding the "traditional" and historically respected view of liberty of conscience that has been upheld throughout Western history.[14]

Yet Hobbes's *instilled conscience* reminds us that the intractable implications of liberty of conscience are hardly unprecedented. In fact, this is the precise reason that Hobbes condemns it so strongly. While Hobbes is known for endorsing a minimal freedom of inward conscience, his vehemence for conscience reveals that he shares Milton's view that liberty of conscience requires far more than a minimal freedom of inward belief. Each individual fashions himself a king, Hobbes warns, emboldening dissenters to do whatever they want rather than obey the law. Justice Antonin Scalia eerily echoes Hobbes and his Erastian contemporaries in the landmark Supreme Court case, *Employment Division* v. *Smith*. Exemptions "in effect,"

[12] NeJaime and Siegel, "Conscience Wars," 2516–2591.
[13] Ibid., 1.
[14] Mancini and Rosenfeld, *The Conscience Wars*, 2.

Scalia warns, "permit every citizen to become a law unto himself."[15] Scalia even enlists the language of "anarchy" to describe appeals to liberty of conscience, reaffirming Hobbes's anxiety about the breakdown of civil uniformity and social cohesion. Stutzman's refusal to design floral arrangements for a same-sex wedding defies the laws of Washington state, thereby undermining the democratic rule of law which all citizens are obligated to accept for a political system to work. Rather than obey the law, Stutzman wants to obey her conscience. The conflict between Stutzman and Ingersoll, as well as the broader "conscience wars" of which this controversy is a part, is evidence of the intuition underlying Hobbes's hostility toward liberty of conscience; liberty of conscience undermines the state.

History seems to have corroborated this Hobbesian insight. Liberty of conscience has been weaponized throughout American history to justify all kinds of injustices and inequities. For example, white Christians invoked liberty of conscience during the Civil Rights Movement to resist efforts to secure racial equality. In *Newman* v. *Piggie*, Maurice Besieger, a Baptist man who led the National Association for the Preservation of White People, argued that his religious beliefs compelled him to refuse service to Black customers at his BBQ restaurants.[16] Commentators insist that recent invocations of conscience are unprecedented, but Hobbes views liberty of conscience as fundamentally intractable.

Perhaps competing consciences are unimportant. It might not necessarily matter what individuals believe as long as they comply with the law. For example, it might not matter if Stutzman's conscience views marriage as an institution between a man and a woman if she does not refuse to provide services to same-sex couples for their weddings or advocates for legislation that advances a specific view of marriage. The fact that Stutzman holds this specific view might be disappointing or disturbing to other American citizens, but it might

---

[15] *Employment Division v. Smith.*, 494 U.S. 872 (1990).
[16] *Newman v. Piggie Park Enterprises, Inc.*, 390 U.S. 400 (1968).

not necessarily matter if her beliefs are not enacted in the world. Yet Hobbes argues that dissenters do not willingly comply with laws that conflict with their conscience. Hobbes's *instilled conscience* anticipates Stutzman's refusal to work with Ingersoll. Even Hobbes – a figure known for enlisting distinctions between belief and action to delineate the scope of sovereignty and authority – recognizes the fragility of this distinction in practice. Dissenters cannot be left alone to believe whatever they want because those beliefs inevitably spill out into the public sphere through our actions and attempts to make those beliefs realized in the world. Conscience prevents dissenters from willingly complying with the law.

Hobbes's *instilled conscience* views invocations to conscience as mere assertions of opinion – deeply held and felt, such that individuals insist on acting in accordance with them, but opinions nonetheless. Hobbes's vehement rejection of conscience invites us to reflect on the origins of conscience in the first place. Hobbes sees, arguably more clearly than many of his contemporaries, that conscience is not fostered in a vacuum, but is reflective of the institutions that shape us – our families, schools, communities, and houses of worship. Stutzman invokes her conscience, but where does her conscience come from? Hobbes recognizes that early modern appeals to conscience are reflective of prevailing religious institutions in our society, and Stutzman's conscientious view of marriage seems similarly shaped and informed by her Baptist upbringing and affiliation. Conscience is instilled by the forces in our world, and so the question at the center of these controversies is not whether Stutzman's conscience should be tolerated, but whether political, social, and religious institutions and communities will instill the value of marriage equality in American politics, such that appeals to conscience will abate over time.

While Hobbes sees nothing but the dangers of liberty of conscience, he also offers us a potential solution to this very problem – civic education – and invites us to consider how we might cultivate consensus, especially on the most important issues. In order to resolve the intractable politics of conscience, Hobbes argues, the state must work to change people's minds and hearts. To thwart resistance to same-sex marriage in civil society, activists and policymakers cannot merely work to pass anti-discrimination laws and policies. The state must also educate American citizens about sexuality, autonomy, and ultimately the meaning of marriage to prevent conscientious appeals against these anti-discrimination laws. The possibility of peaceful coexistence becomes, at some point, about the project of persuasion.

Hobbes's account of *instilled conscience* might seem discouraging in our deeply partisan and divisive political climate and for good reason. Individuals like Stutzman feel bound to their conscience, and many invocations of conscience in American society are fundamentally incompatible with one another. It might also seem too idealistic, assuming that meaningful social change is possible in a world in which division has been exacerbated in recent decades and radical views find an outlet in fringe spaces in civil society and on social media. Critics might be skeptical that civic education can change the mind of someone like Stutzman, especially about something so important like marriage. But our deeply divided world is arguably evidence, Hobbes might suggest, of our need for civic education. After all, competing claims of conscience in contemporary politics – for example, a florist who refuses to make floral arrangements for a same-sex wedding – are demonstrative of a competing understanding of the institution of marriage and individual autonomy. Unlike Spinoza and Bayle who accept the inevitable disadvantages of conscience in their attempt to liberate it, Hobbes aims to offer a potential solution to the unruly effect of conscience in politics – eliminate it altogether.

Hobbes's approach to conscience, on the other hand, might feel draconian. After all, it attempts to eradicate difference rather than considering how best to respond to the inevitable facts of pluralism, as Rawls would later call them. This approach to conscience might ensure that competing claims of conscience abate over time, but it also requires more severe and invasive policies and approaches to conscience. We might caution that the state, especially the American state with its longstanding history of oppression and imperialism, might not be able to design and disseminate such an inclusive civic education. At the same time, Hobbes urges us to consider that civic education *will* happen, one way or another, with other institutions filling this void. In early modern England, Hobbes recognized that other institutions – rather than the state – operate in this role. If American democracy hopes to have a fighting chance at cultivating some degree of consensus on crucial social and political issues, we should heed Hobbes's counsel to think carefully about where conscience comes from in the first place rather than focusing exclusively on what to do when it manifests itself in politics.

Contemporary accounts of toleration in political theory often focus on the problem of difference and disagreement – how to talk to one another despite our immense differences – but Spinoza warns of an overlooked yet critical aspect of social relationships: sincerity. On his account, it matters very little how we talk to one another if our outward expressions are merely an act of hypocritical conformity. By stressing the significance of sincerity and authenticity in cultivating trust, Spinoza complicates the standard question at the heart of debates on toleration. He does not ask how much difference we can bear or how much respect we owe to those who are different than us; rather, he argues that the toleration of dissent is not necessarily a problem to be overcome but rather the very foundation of political freedom. We may be tempted, fairly enough, to suppress certain kinds of speech, either through self-censorship or political regulation, to avert the consequences of that speech in civil society, but Spinoza warns that regulations of speech – while successful in squashing disagreement – have their own detrimental consequences on social relationships. Hypocritical conformity has its own pernicious consequences that must be balanced against the harm done by conscience. This view does not hinge on the sanctity of conscience, but a recognition that the state's refusal to protect liberty of conscience, to some extent, makes us hypocrites, unable to trust that the

124 THE POLITICS OF CONSCIENCE

words of our political leaderships and fellow citizens are, relatively, representative of their actual beliefs. The alternative – ubiquitous distrust – thwarts the very foundation of mutual understanding and shared reality which are necessary for freedom. This is hardly a principled defense of toleration, but a recognition that some degree of authenticity, frankness, and trust are necessary for society to function and allow for the conditions of freedom.

A Spinozist approach to *Arlene's Flowers* might suggest that Stutzman should not be exempted from Washington's antidiscrimination laws and allowed to refuse service to a same-sex couple for wedding floral arrangement or that Stutzman must be willing to bear the burden of the punishment for breaking the antidiscrimination law. Yet it might also maintain that Stutzman should be allowed to post signage in her storefront or on her website about her preference for working with opposite-sex clients on wedding floral arrangements. It might also suggest that Stutzman should be allowed to criticize the lack of accommodation of her conscience publicly, even if doing so would inflict its own harm. Stutzman must be free to express her conscience because if each citizen cannot trust that the words of others are nothing but feigned conformity to the law, the very fabric of society breaks down. Spinoza's *conscientious speech* does not suggest that we should be concerned with the sanctity of Stutzman's conscience, but with the fractured fabric of civil society if her conscience is not freely expressed.

There are clear advantages and disadvantages to a Spinozist approach to liberty of conscience. Spinoza's *conscientious speech* might seem far too limited, failing to restrict hate and vitriol in public discourse and spaces at precisely a moment in which hate and vitriol are on the rise. Even commentators on opposing sides of the contemporary debate on hate speech recognize the dignitarian harms inflicted by offensive speech.[17] Stutzman's *conscientious speech*

---

[17] Jeremy Waldron, *The Harm in Hate Speech* (Cambridge, MA: Harvard University Press, 2012); Teresa Bejan, *Mere Civility: Toleration and Its Limits in Early Modern England and America* (Cambridge, MA: Harvard University Press, 2017).

III   *ARLENE'S FLOWERS* AND THE PSYCHOLOGY OF CONSCIENCE   125

would inflict dignitarian harm on Ingersoll and undermine democratic and egalitarian norms and laws, even if the state remained committed to upholding Washington's anti-discrimination laws. On the other hand, it might seem too strict, curbing a dissenter's ability to combat the perceived injustices of the state with more active forms of resistance.

Yet Spinoza's *conscientious speech* has one clear advantage – its neutrality. It distinguishes speech from action, such that the state does not adjudicate which claims of conscience are too "harmful" to be tolerated. As critics of John Stuart Mill and the harm principle have recognized, "harm" has been invoked throughout American history to justify discrimination and oppression of minoritarian religious traditions. "Comparisons of some new religion's practices of child sacrifice and slavery abound," Martha Nussbaum argues, "when people are gearing up to discriminate against others."[18] Municipalities manipulate zoning laws to obstruct the construction of mosques in certain neighborhoods or forbid Muslim employees from wearing headscarves, but these infringements are not actually demonstrative of a commitment to public safety or civil order, as their proponents suggest, but of anti-Islamic sentiment. Infringements on liberty of conscience are, of course, justified in certain cases, but we should also recognize that they are often arbitrary and discriminatory. By shifting the limits of toleration from harm to speech, the Spinozist approach fails to restrict harmful and hurtful speech from public discourse and spaces while also assuring the neutrality of restrictions on religion.

While Spinoza draws attention to the social dynamics of hypocritical conformity, Bayle considers the psychological effects of conformity on the dissenter himself as well as the counterintuitive implications of this infringement. Bayle's *tormented conscience* suggests that infringements on conscience are experienced as deep

---

[18] Martha Nussbaum, *Liberty of Conscience: In Defense of America's Tradition of Religious Equality* (New York: Basic Books, 2008), 24.

126 THE POLITICS OF CONSCIENCE

violations by dissenters. Political and social pressures to conform, especially when dissimulation includes a refusal of conscience that is deeply destructive to an individual's sense of identity, are perhaps just as unsettling as more violent forms of discipline and coercion. The experience of conforming does not merely corrode mutual understanding among democratic citizens, as Spinoza suggests, but also asks individuals to endure the psychologically taxing experience of suppressing conscience. Bayle describes this as an experience of falsehood or imposture by the dissenter. Hypocritical conformity is not merely a trivial demand with little consequence for integrity but a deeply felt violation that troubles the dissenter long after the act of conformity is complete. Bayle's *tormented conscience* accounts well for the psychological conflict as described by Stutzman's refusal. Bayle helps us appreciate why Stutzman finds this decision to be immensely taxing; conforming to the anti-discrimination law is painful for her, even while acknowledging that she is concerned for Ingersoll. Bayle helps us appreciate the very real and deeply felt burden of conscience on figures like Stutzman. Bayle's *tormented conscience* and the psychological strain of infringements on conscience do not necessarily justify exempting Stutzman from the law, but they do urge us to consider the psychological damage done by hypocritical conformity.

Even more discerningly, Bayle recognizes that violations of conscience tend to exacerbate fervor. Hypocritical conformity does not inspire genuine conversion but tends to radicalize dissenters and attach them even more deeply to their conscience, which is all the more troubling in a world in which so many continue to preach hate and vitriol. In an attempt to create a more inclusive society, American laws and policies promote equality among democratic citizens. The social norms of civility and political correctness pressure American citizens into concealing their discriminatory beliefs and limiting public expressions of hostility and prejudice. Such pretense and prevarication play an essential role in preserving at least the outward semblance of civility and decorum in civil society, even if disingenuous. The social scientist Jon Elster hoped this process of

III *ARLENE'S FLOWERS* AND THE PSYCHOLOGY OF CONSCIENCE 127

conformity would change the minds of citizens, what he called the "civilizing" effect of hypocrisy.[19] Yet some American citizens have been angered by demands for their conformity to principles of equality and inclusion and doubled down on their values of exclusion and prejudice. This remains to be seen in the example of Stutzman. Will Stutzman double down on her refusal to work with same-sex couples? Will she encourage others to do the same? Or beyond Stutzman, will she inspire a backlash against marriage equality? This Baylean intuition does not necessarily tell us where to draw the limits of toleration – what should be tolerated and what goes beyond the pale – but it does tell us something about what to expect when we deem something intolerable.

Bayle's *tormented conscience* suggests that we should approach conscience with respect and empathy rather than disdain and disparagement. Even if certain practices are deemed intolerable, it is important that dissenters feel that they have been perceived as legitimate to mitigate pushback and potential radicalization. The politics of toleration is not only about what is ultimately allowed, but also how we approach that which is deemed intolerable. There are many compelling reasons, for example, why Stutzman's refusal should not be accommodated, but we can also treat this decision as a meaningful infringement on her conscience. Something is lost when we call on American citizens to comply, to compromise, and to conform, even if this conformity is ultimately the right thing to do to uphold democratic equality and protect marginalized members of American society. This does not mean that all conscientious dissent should be accommodated. But it does mean that invocations of conscience should be treated with dignity and that the internal conflict that conscientious dissenters face should be recognized. As Chad Flanders argues, Washington state does this well in *Arlene's Flowers* by treating Stutzman's conscience with respect and attempting to resolve

---

[19] Jon Elster, "Deliberation and Constitution Making," in *Deliberative Democracy*, ed. Jon Elster (Cambridge: Cambridge University Press, 1998), 97–122.

128   THE POLITICS OF CONSCIENCE

this conflict with care for both parties. Yet an acknowledgment of this burden on a dissenter does not necessarily mean eliminating it. Or put otherwise, "recognition is not accommodation."[20] But this recognition might abate some degree of the radicalization that can happen when conscience is not tolerated. It is important to be honest about these costs, not merely because of intellectual honesty or integrity, but because attempts to erase them, as Bayle stresses, exacerbate resentment and attach dissenters even more fervently to their conscience.

Ruth Bader Ginsberg eerily echoes Bayle in her Madison Lecture series at New York University, in which she argues that abrupt and radical social and political change often inspires enormous backlash and slows progress.[21] She offers up the example of reproductive freedom in American politics and suggests that the legalization of abortion in *Roe* v. *Wade* emboldened anti-choice advocates. While *Roe* afforded women access to life-affirming reproductive healthcare, Ginsberg suggests that it also "halted" progress and "prolonged divisiveness and deferred stable settlement of the issue" into the twenty-first century.[22] Even Ginsberg, a fierce advocate for women's rights, suggests that drastic social change "risk[s] a backlash too forceful to contain," thereby undermining the very goal it aims to secure.[23] In one pithy and alarming warning, Ginsberg advocates for a more moderate view of political change: "doctrinal limbs too swiftly shaped, experience teaches, may prove unstable."[24] Ginsberg's advocacy for more "measured motions" is arguably an unpopular view;

---

[20] Chad Flanders and Sean Oliveira, "Whose Conscience? Which Complicity? Reconciling Burdens and Interests in the Law of Religious Liberty," in *Law and Religion in the Liberal State*, eds. Jahid Hossain Bhuiyan and Darryn Jensen (New York: Bloomsbury, 2020), 174. Flanders makes a slightly different point to the Baylean one, suggesting that by refusing to recognize the meaningful burden imposed on Stutzman, we fail to recognize the depth of the state's interest in promoting anti-discrimination and equality among democratic citizens.

[21] Ruth Bader Ginsburg, "Speaking in a Judicial Voice," *New York University Law Review* 67, no. 6 (1992): 1185–1209.

[22] Ibid., 1208.

[23] Ibid.

[24] Ibid., 1198.

III ARLENE'S FLOWERS AND THE PSYCHOLOGY OF CONSCIENCE 129

the stakes of reproductive freedom, like the politics of conscience, are immensely high, and slower progress means inequality and death, especially for marginalized women and birthing people, in the meantime.[25] Yet Bayle's *tormented conscience* warns that considerable and rapid change might create a more polarizing environment, inspire enormous backlash, and counterintuitively thwart the very progress that advocates are seeking in the long-run.

This recognition of the psychological implications of liberty of conscience should not be read, full-stop, as suggesting that all outward expressions should be tolerated. There are many compelling reasons why we might not want to tolerate certain rituals or forms of expression, even despite our acknowledgment that the strict regulation of these outward behaviors might infringe on conscience. Like Hobbes and Spinoza, we might view some forms of outward dissent and conduct as too incendiary or oppressive to deserve accommodation. Yet it does suggest that we cannot argue that no harm is done to Stutzman when we ask her to comply with the anti-discrimination law. As Robert Visher notes, the liberal solution to the problem of difference – the distinction of belief from action – often insists that no harm is done by asking the dissenter to conform.[26] Liberals imagine that they can "leav[e] untouched the idiosyncratic and seemingly archaic worldviews of individuals and groups while avoiding the tangible harms that arise from actions driven by those worldviews."[27] The four early modern figures in this project, even Hobbes who is known for defending this view, question this logic. Erasing the psychological harm of hypocritical conformity, Bayle warns, may do more harm than if we would acknowledge the infringement on conscience. To the extent that Bayle has emerged as the hero of this book, it is this enduring insight into liberty of conscience and hypocritical conformity that has earned him this status.

---

[25] Ibid.

[26] Robert Vischer, *Conscience and the Common Good: Reclaiming the Space between Person and State* (Cambridge: Cambridge University Press, 2009), 99.

[27] Ibid.

130 THE POLITICS OF CONSCIENCE

These four early modern figures urge us to broaden our understanding of the stakes of *Arlene's Flowers* beyond the balancing act between religious freedom and liberty of conscience, on the one hand, and democratic equality, on the other. Milton's *expressive conscience* suggests that the delicate balancing act between conscience and other political commitments need not be imagined as a zero-sum game; there are degrees of concession that might be extended to dissenters and compromises worth pursuing. Hobbes's *instilled conscience* urges us to consider where conscience comes from in the first place and strategies to abate it, long before it manifests in now-familiar controversies on the proper role of religion in democratic politics. Spinoza's *conscientious speech* invites us to reflect on the ways that limits on toleration frustrate the very possibility of social trust and political freedom. While political correctness, for example, thwarts the outward expression of prejudice, it also cultivates a culture of distrust since we never know for certain if we are interacting with friend or foe, especially after it has been exposed as mere pretense. And finally, Bayle's *tormented conscience* suggests that debates on liberty of conscience should not be merely concerned with whether conscience should or should not be tolerated, but with how we should approach conscience to avoid its intensification. These four figures urge us to think beyond the narrow framing of the balancing act between Stutzman's conscience and Ingersoll's right to equality to attend to these other crucial, yet underexamined, political, social, and psychological dynamics.

IV *WARREN* AND THE PROGRESSIVE POLITICS OF CONSCIENCE

United States v. *Warren* challenges many of our intuitions from *Arlene's Flowers* and deepens our appreciation of the role of conscience in progressive American politics. In the broader context of increasingly militarized borders, sanctuary city crackdowns, and the criminalization of migrant solidarity, Méadhbh McIvor argues, Scott Warren emerges as an example of the kind of progressive politics that

IV WARREN AND THE PROGRESSIVE POLITICS OF CONSCIENCE 131

might be advanced by liberty of conscience.[28] Warren is a lecturer at Arizona State University and a humanitarian aid worker collaborating with the faith-based border aid group, No More Deaths (No Más Muertes), a ministry of the Unitarian Universalist Church in Tucson, Arizona. Warren's case is notable since it interrupts the prevailing view that religious freedom and liberty of conscience are "associated with the Christian right."[29] As McIvor stresses, the "recognition of Warren's spiritual beliefs as equivalent to those of conservative Christians" is "groundbreaking."[30] Yet, like Stutzman, Warren's actions urge us to grapple with the implications and limits of liberty of conscience in practice.

This second case concerns a humanitarian aid worker, Scott Warren, who provided food, water, and temporary shelter to two undocumented migrants, Kristian Perez Villanueva of El Salvador and José Arnaldo Sacaria-Goday of Honduras, crossing the US–Mexico border. Warren acts in accordance with his conscience to protect these "migrants who [found] themselves in distress" in the dangerous Arizona desert.[31] Many volunteers with this organization describe themselves as "people of conscience" acting to curb human rights violations by the American government.[32] Warren's legal defense hinges, in part, on an appeal to liberty of conscience. Warren insists that his conscience compelled him to "respon[d] to the humanitarian crisis" by offering aid to migrants.[33] His first trial results in a mistrial due to a gridlocked jury, and he is later acquitted of all charges in a second trial.

Our first-blush reaction to Warren's resistance might be one of support as his conscience advances human solidarity and human

---

[28] Méadhbh McIvor, "Water in the Desert," *Anthropology News*, https://anthropology-news.org/index.php/2020/12/11/water-in-the-desert/, 2020.

[29] Ibid.

[30] Ibid.

[31] Scott Warren, "In Defense of Wilderness: Policing Public Borderlands," *South Atlantic Quarterly* (2017) 116 (4): 863.

[32] Ibid., 863.

[33] Ibid., 870.

rights in the face of "violent" and "destructive" militarized border measures.[34] Warren's support for human dignity and open borders arguably provokes a different reaction than Stutzman's appeal to conscience, understandable given her Baptist background, yet counter to human dignity. By invoking liberty of conscience to resist harmful immigration policies that push marginalized individuals into unsafe terrain and certain death, Warren offers a different account of the politics of conscience. Milton's *expressive conscience*, again, urges us to consider minimizing infringements on Warren's conscience. Warren's conscience should be protected in this case, affording him the right to deliver food and supplies to vulnerable populations in the Arizona desert. His humanitarian work, and the broader humanitarian efforts of No More Deaths, should be exempt from the immigration law. In the balancing act between safeguarding the conscience of activists and securing the border, conscience should prevail. At the very least, Milton's *expressive conscience* urges us to consider strategies to safeguard Warren's conscience, while also securing immigration policies.

Hobbes's *instilled conscience*, on the other hand, encourages us to reconsider our initial reaction to Warren's violation of the law. By violating U.S. immigration laws, or any law really, Warren undermines American democracy, suggesting that laws only apply in certain situations or to certain individuals. The immigration law, which prohibits the harboring of undocumented aliens, might be an unjust law, but it is still the law. The four jurors who were unwilling to acquit Warren in his first trial affirmed this Hobbesian view. Hobbes's *instilled conscience* stresses that dissenters act in accordance with their conscience rather than the law, and Warren's humanitarian aid furthers defiance. Warren treats his conscience as the law rather than the actual immigration law; he is, simply put, unwilling to accept the laws of his state. Warren also corroborates Hobbes's insight that dissenters will not willingly comply with the

---

[34] Scott Warren, "In Defense of Wilderness," 871.

IV *WARREN* AND THE PROGRESSIVE POLITICS OF CONSCIENCE 133

law. Warren reiterates throughout his public essays that he and other "solidarity workers" will "continue to act" despite the legal repercussions of their actions.[35] The distinction between belief and action collapses under the burden of Warren's conscience.

Hobbes's vehement critique of conscience invites us to consider whether we should reject Warren's commitment to his conscience – which leads him to break the law – but it also invites us to consider how to cultivate consensus on an issue as polarizing as immigration in American politics. There is the question of whether it is reasonable to expect Warren to act against his conscience, even if it means violating the democratic laws of the state, but there is also a broader question about the possibility of social and legal change. What role might civic education play in changing social norms such that changes in political and legal norms might follow? This broader project of social transformation is crucial, not only to convince dissenters like Warren to comply – or not comply – with the law, but also to change civil society. After all, the story of Warren's case does not only concern Warren himself, but also involves the members of the two juries that participated in his trials. In the end, civic education must be wide-reaching and comprehensive to affect the conscience of all American citizens.

Spinoza's *conscientious speech* asks us to reflect on a potential compromise between these two approaches. Like Hobbes, Spinoza appreciates that liberty of conscience implics political and social turmoil. After all, Warren disobeys the law, even if his conscience motivates humanitarian work. Warren cannot be free to do whatever he likes, Spinoza might insist, even if his conscience conflicts with the law; this would amount to chaos in practice. Yet Spinoza's *conscientious speech* might also recognize that Warren's conformity with oppressive immigration policies thwarts potential collaborations with other dissenters and undermines civic trust among Warren and

---

[35] Scott Warren, "Borders and the Freedom to Move," *Dialogues in Human Geography* 9, no. 3 (2019): 225.

his fellow citizens. If Warren complies with these policies, his conformity might be interpreted as acquiescence by others in his community, breaking down potential collaborations and coordination of resistance against unjust immigration policies. Others cannot truly know Warren and his progressive conscientious views in an authentic way, such that the possibility of mutual recognition and civic trust among Warren and other citizens is obscured. Spinoza's *conscientious speech* aims to resolve this issue by suggesting that dissenters must conform to the law, even if it conflicts with their conscience, while also insisting they should be able to express their conscience freely in speech. A Spinozist approach to Warren's case, therefore, might suggest that he comply with the immigration laws, even if that conformity violates his conscience, yet be free to speak openly and actively against these laws. Warren cannot be allowed to provide food and shelter to undocumented migrants in the Arizona desert, but the state cannot restrict his loud critiques of these policies.

The implications of Spinoza's *conscientious speech* might seem negligible, especially in the case of Warren's humanitarian aid. By allowing him to speak out against these laws but restricting his humanitarian aid effort to the migrants, the Spinozist approach to conscience fails to offer Warren a more active route to combat the perceived injustice of the American state. Yet it remains neutral to conscience. The state is not asked to adjudicate the difference between Stutzman and Warren and their claims of conscience. While this certainly restricts conscientious action, it also ensures that the state does not privilege certain appeals to conscience while restricting others.

Spinoza stresses the potential thwarting of social connections and collaborations, but Bayle's *tormented conscience* sheds light on the psychological damage inflicted on the dissenter himself. Bayle recognizes, arguably more clearly than his contemporaries, that conformity is experienced as a deep violation by the dissenter. Warren's conformity, we should anticipate, violates him in a meaningful way. Demanding that Warren curb his humanitarian impulse and restrict his support for those suffering would be psychologically harrowing for him. It would violate Warren's understanding of himself as an individual. Hypocritical conformity would not be a straightforward, simple demand of Warren, but is felt as a serious infringement. Perhaps this turmoil might be productive, inciting Warren and others in No More Deaths to double down on their efforts; but it surely will not arouse ambivalence.

Warren's conscience reminds us that there are many examples of religious actors and activists whose conscience furthers a more progressive vision of politics, including individuals who officiate weddings for same-sex couples, protest the death penalty, and pursue environmental justice. By continuing to focus exclusively on figures like Jack Phillips, we overlook controversies on the migrant, the prisoner, and the Muslim that deserve our attention. Many religious minorities, such as Jews, Sikhs, Muslims, Black Christians, and Indigenous communities, remain vulnerable, especially now that the "culture wars [have] erod[ed] support for religious liberty."[36] As scholars at the Law, Rights, and Religion Project at Columbia Law School have argued, the "right wing Christians' troubling successful capture of 'religious liberty' has resulted in the rapid erosion rather than protection of this right."[37] Christian evangelicals have too heavily dominated popular discourse, while other cases of religious intolerance have been overlooked – a crucial problem given the upsurge of anti-Semitism, anti-Muslim, and anti-immigrant sentiment across America. Milton reminds us of a simple, yet crucial acknowledgment that is all too easily forgotten today – toleration does not necessarily signal the end of intolerance. This is hardly a novel insight, but it is surely one that bears repeating in a historical moment in which Christian evangelicals receive protection while a presidential

---

[36] Laycock, "Religious Liberty and the Culture Wars," 876.

[37] Elizabeth Reiner Platt, Katherine Franke, Kira Shepherd, and Lilia Hadjiivanova, "Whose Faith Matters? The Fight for Religious Liberty beyond the Christian Right." *Columbia Law School, Law, Rights, and Religion Project*, November 2019, https://lawrightsreligion.law.columbia.edu/sites/default/files/content/Images/Whose%20Faith%20Matters%20Full%20Report%2012.12.19.pdf.

administration advances a Muslim ban. To the extent that liberty of conscience has become contested once more, this book argues that this crucial freedom remains central to realizing political freedom. Liberty of conscience remains a powerful tool to promote toleration in American society and safeguard the freedom of vulnerable religious individuals and communities. To call on Milton, then a young aspiring poet, one final time, "Give me the liberty to know, to utter, and to argue freely according to conscience, above all liberties" (CPW 2.560).

Bibliography

Abizadeh, Arash. "Hobbes on the Causes of War: A Disagreement Theory." *American Political Science Review* 105, no. 2 (2011): 298–315.

Abizadeh, Arash. "Publicity, Privacy, and Religious Toleration in Hobbes' Leviathan." *Modern Intellectual History* 10, no. 2 (2013): 261–291.

Achinstein, Sharon. *Milton and the Revolutionary Reader*. Princeton: Princeton University Press, 1994.

Achinstein, Sharon, and Elizabeth Sauer, eds. *Milton and Toleration*. Oxford: Oxford University Press, 2007.

Anderson, Jeremy. "The Role of Education in Political Stability." *Hobbes Studies* 16, no. 1 (2003): 95–104,

Armitage, David, Armand Himy, and Quentin Skinner, eds. *Milton and Republicanism*. Cambridge: Cambridge University Press, 1995.

Asad, Talal. *Formations of the Secular: Christianity, Islam, Modernity*. Palo Alto: Stanford University Press, 2003.

Asad, Talal. "Thinking about Religion, Belief, and Politics." In *Cambridge Companion to Religious Studies*, edited by Robert Orsi, 36–57. Cambridge: Cambridge University Press, 2012.

Asad, Talal, Wendy Brown, Judith Butler, and Saba Mahmood. *Is Critique Secular? Blasphemy, Injury, and Free Speech*. New York: Fordham University Press, 2013.

Bayle, Pierre. *A Philosophical Commentary on These Words of the Gospel, Luke 14.23, "Compel Them to Come In, That My House May Be Full."* Edited by John Kilcullen and Chandran Kukathas. Indianapolis: Liberty Fund, 2005.

Beiner, Ronald. "Three Versions of the Politics of Conscience: Hobbes, Spinoza, Locke." *San Diego Law Review* 47, no. 3 (2010): 1107–1134.

Beiner, Ronald. *Civil Religion: A Dialogue in the History of Political Philosophy*. Cambridge: Cambridge University Press, 2010.

Bejan, Teresa. "Difference without Disagreement: Rethinking Hobbes on 'Independency' and Toleration." *Review of Politics* 78, no. 1 (2016): 1–25.

Bejan, Teresa. "First Impressions: Hobbes on Religion, Education, and the Metaphor of Imprinting." In *Hobbes on Politics and Religion*, edited by Laurens van Apeldoorn and Robin Douglass, 45–62. Oxford: Oxford University Press, 2018.

BIBLIOGRAPHY

Bejan, Teresa. "Recent Work on Toleration." *Review of Politics* 80, no. 4 (2018): 701–708.

Bejan, Teresa. "Teaching the *Leviathan*: Thomas Hobbes on Education." *Oxford Review of Education* 36, no. 5 (2010): 607–626.

Bejan, Teresa. *Mere Civility: Disagreement and the Limits of Toleration.* Cambridge, MA: Harvard University Press, 2017.

Blinder, Alan, and Richard Pérez-Peña. "Kentucky Clerk Denies Same-Sex Marriage Licenses, Defying Court." *New York Times.* Accessed September 1, 2015. www.nytimes.com/2015/09/02/us/same-sex-marriage-kentucky-kim-davis.html.

Bowlin, John. *Tolerance among the Virtues.* Princeton: Princeton University Press, 2016.

Braun, Harald, and Edward Vallance, eds. *Context of Conscience in Early Modern Europe, 1500–1700.* New York: Palgrave Macmillan, 2004.

Brown, Wendy. *Regulating Aversion: Tolerance in the Age of Identity and Empire.* Princeton: Princeton University Press, 2008.

Cable, Lana. "Secularizing Conscience in Milton's Republican Community." In *Milton and Toleration*, edited by Sharon Achinstein and Elizabeth Sauer, 268–283. Oxford: Oxford University Press, 2007.

Coffey, John. *Persecution and Toleration in Protestant England, 1558–1689.* London: Harlow, 2000.

Coffey, John. "Milton, Locke, and the New History of Toleration." *Modern Intellectual History* 5, no. 3 (2008): 619–632.

Collins, Jeffrey. "Redeeming the Enlightenment: New Histories of Religious Toleration." *The Journal of Modern History* 81, no. 3 (2009): 607–636.

Collins, Jeffrey. *The Allegiance of Thomas Hobbes.* Oxford: Oxford University Press, 2005.

Cooper, Julie. "Freedom of Speech and Philosophical Citizenship in Spinoza's Theologico-Political Treatise." *Law, Culture, and the Humanities* 2, no. 1 (2006): 91–114.

Cooper, Julie. *Secular Powers: Humility in Modern Political Thought.* Chicago: University of Chicago Press, 2013.

Dobranski, Stephen, and John Rumrich, eds. *Milton and Heresy.* Cambridge: Cambridge University Press, 1998.

Dunn, John. *The Political Thought of John Locke.* Cambridge: Cambridge University Press, 1969.

Dunn, John. "The Concept of Trust in the Politics of John Locke." In *Philosophy in History: Essays on the Historiography of Philosophy*, edited by Richard Rorty, Jerome Schneewind, and Quentin Skinner, 279–302. Cambridge: Cambridge University Press, 1984.

BIBLIOGRAPHY

Dunn, John. "The Claim to Freedom of Conscience: Freedom of Speech, Freedom of Thought, Freedom of Worship." In *From Persecution to Toleration: The Glorious Revolution and Religion in England*, edited by Ole Peter Grell, Jonathan Israel, and Nicholas Tyacke, 171–193. Oxford: Oxford University Press, 1991.

Eisgruber, Christopher, and Lawrence Sagar. *Religious Freedom and the Constitution*. Cambridge, MA: Harvard University Press, 2007.

Elster, Jon. "Deliberation and Constitution Making." In *Deliberative Democracy*, edited by Jon Elster, 97–122. Cambridge: Cambridge University Press, 1998.

Feldman, Noah. *Divided by God: America's Church-State Problem – And What We Should Do about It*. New York: Farrar, Straus, and Giroux, 2006.

Fish, Stanley. *How Milton Works*. Cambridge, MA: Harvard University Press, 2001.

Flanders, Chad, and Sean Oliveira. "Whose Conscience? Which Complicity? Reconciling Burdens and Interests in the Law of Religious Liberty." In *Law and Religion in the Liberal State*, edited by Jahid Hossain Bhuiyan and Darryn Jensen, 161–176. New York: Bloomsbury, 2020.

Forst, Rainer. "Pierre Bayle's Reflective Theory of Toleration." In *Toleration and Its Limits*, edited by Melissa Williams and Jeremy Waldron, 78–113. New York: NYU Press, 2008.

Forst, Rainer. "Religion, Reason, and Toleration: Bayle, Kant – And Us." In *Religion and Liberal Political Philosophy*, edited by Cécile Laborde and Aurelia Bardon, 249–261. Oxford: Oxford University Press, 2017.

Forst, Rainer. *Toleration in Conflict: Past and Present*. Cambridge: Cambridge University Press, 2013.

Freed, Curt, and Robert Ingersoll. "Why We Sued Our Favorite Florist: Marriage Equality Must Be Truly Equal." *Seattle Times*. Accessed March 1, 2021. www .seattletimes.com/opinionwhy-true-marriage-equality-matters-to-us.

Gais, Amy. "The Politics of Hypocrisy: Baruch Spinoza and Pierre Bayle on Hypocritical Conformity." *Political Theory* 48, no. 5 (2020): 588–614.

Gais, Amy. "Thomas Hobbes and 'Gently Instilled' Conscience." *History of European Ideas* 47, no. 8 (2021): 1211–1227.

Gandhi, Mahatma. *Selected Political Writings*. Edited by Dennis Dalton. Indianapolis, IN: Hackett, 1996.

Garsten, Bryan. *Saving Persuasion: A Defense of Rhetoric and Judgment*. Cambridge, MA: Harvard University Press, 2006.

George, Robert P., and Sherif Girgis. "A Baker's First Amendment Rights." *New York Times*. Accessed May 1, 2018. www.nytimes.com/2017/12/04/opinion first-amendment-wedding-cake.html.

Goldie, Mark. "The Theory of Intolerance in Restoration Britain." In *From Persecution to Toleration: The Glorious Revolution and Religion in England*,

BIBLIOGRAPHY

edited by Ole Peter Grell, Jonathan Israel, and Nicholas Tyacke, 331–368. Oxford: Clarendon Press, 1991.

Hadfield, Andrew. "Milton and Catholicism." In *Milton and Toleration*, edited by Sharon Achinstein and Elizabeth Sauer, 186–202. Oxford: Oxford University Press, 2007.

Hadfield, Andrew. *Lying in Early Modern English Culture: From the Oath of Supremacy to the Oath of Allegiance*. Oxford: Oxford University Press, 2017.

Hanin, Mark. "Thomas Hobbes's Theory of Conscience." *History of Political Thought* 33, no. 1 (2012): 55–85.

Henry, Julie. "Freedom of Conscience in Spinoza's Political Treatise: Between Sovereign Limitations and Citizen Demand." *Reformation and Renaissance Review* 14, no. 1 (2012): 8–22.

Hobbes, Thomas. *Behemoth, or Long Parliament*. Edited by Ferdinand Tönnies. Chicago: University of Chicago Press, 1990.

Hobbes, Thomas. *De Cive*. Edited by Richard Tuck and Michael Silverthorne. New York: Cambridge University Press, 1998.

Hobbes, Thomas. *Thomas Hobbes: Leviathan, Volume 2*. Edited by Noel Malcolm. Oxford: Clarendon Press, 2012.

Hoekstra, Kinch. "The End of Philosophy (The Case of Hobbes)." *Proceedings of the Aristotelian Society* 106, no. 1 (2006): 25–62.

Hughes, Ann. "Afterword." In *Milton and Toleration*, edited by Sharon Achinstein and Elizabeth Sauer, 299–304. Oxford: Oxford University Press, 2007.

Israel, Jonathan. *Radical Enlightenment: Philosophy and the Making of Modernity, 1650–1750*. Oxford: Oxford University Press, 2001.

Israel, Jonathan. *Enlightenment Contested: Philosophy, Modernity, and the Emancipation of Man, 1670–1752*. Oxford: Oxford University Press, 2006.

James, Susan. *Spinoza on Philosophy, Religion, and Politics: The Theologico-Political Treatise*. Oxford: Oxford University Press, 2012.

Johnston, David. *The Rhetoric of Leviathan: Hobbes and the Politics of Cultural Transformation*. Princeton: Princeton University Press, 1989.

Kahn, Victoria. "The Metaphorical Contract in Milton's Tenure of Kings and Magistrates." In *Milton and Republicanism*, edited by David Armitage, Armand Himy and Quentin Skinner, 82–105. Cambridge: Cambridge University Press, 1995.

Kahn, Victoria. *Machiavellian Rhetoric from the Counter-Reformation to Milton*. Princeton: Princeton University Press, 1994.

Kaplan, Benjamin. *Divided by Faith: Religious Conflict and the Practice of Toleration in Early Modern Europe*. Cambridge, MA: Harvard University Press, 2007.

BIBLIOGRAPHY 141

King, Jr., Martin Luther. "Letter from a Birmingham City Jail." In *A Testament of Hope: The Essential Writings and Speeches of Martin Luther King Jr.*, edited by James Washington. New York: Harper Collins, 1990.

Krom, Michael. *The Limits of Reason in Hobbes's Commonwealth*. New York: Bloomsbury, 2013.

Kukathas, Chandran. "Toleration without Limits: A Reconstruction and Defense of Pierre Bayle's Philosophical Commentary." In *Religion and Liberal Political Philosophy*, edited by Cécile Laborde and Aurelia Bardon, 262–274. Oxford: Oxford University Press, 2017.

Kuran, Timur. *Private Truth, Public Lies: The Social Consequences of Preference Falsification*. Cambridge, MA: Harvard University Press, 1997.

Laborde, Cécile. *Liberalism's Religion*. Cambridge, MA: Harvard University Press, 2017.

Laycock, Douglas. "Religious Liberty and the Culture Wars." *University of Illinois Law Review* 3 (2014): 839–880.

Lewalski, Barbara. *The Life of John Milton*. Malden, MA: Blackwell, 2000.

Lilla, Mark. *The Stillborn God: Religion, Politics, and the Modern West*. New York: Vintage, 2008.

Liptak, Adam. "In Narrow Decision, Supreme Court Sides with Baker Who Turned Away Gay Couple." *New York Times*. Accessed June 4, 2018. www .nytimes.com/2018/06/04/us/politics/supreme-court-sides-with-baker-who-turned-away-gay-couple.html.

Lloyd, Sally A. *Ideals as Interests in Hobbes's Leviathan*. Cambridge: Cambridge University Press, 1992.

Lloyd, Sally A. *Morality in the Philosophy of Thomas Hobbes: Cases in the Law of Nature*. Cambridge: Cambridge University Press, 2009.

Lloyd, Sally A. *Interpreting Hobbes's Political Philosophy*. Cambridge: Cambridge University Press, 2019.

Loewenstein, David. *Treacherous Faith: The Specter of Heresy in Early Modern English Literature and Culture*. Oxford: Oxford University Press, 2013.

Lovett, Frank. "Milton's Case for a Free Commonwealth." *American Journal of Political Science* 49, no. 3 (2005): 466–478.

Maclure, Jocelyn, and Charles Taylor. *Secularism and Freedom of Conscience*. Translated by Jane Marie Todd. Cambridge, MA: Harvard University Press, 2011.

Mahmood, Saba. *Politics of Piety: The Islamic Revival and the Feminist Subject*. Princeton: Princeton University Press, 2011.

Mahmood, Saba. *Religious Difference in a Secular Age: A Minority Report*. Princeton: Princeton University Press, 2015.

Malcolm, Noel. *Aspects of Hobbes*. Oxford: Oxford University Press, 2004.

BIBLIOGRAPHY

Maltzahn, Nicholas von. *Milton's History of Britain: Republican Historiography in the English Revolution.* Oxford: Clarendon Press, 1991.

Maltzahn, Nicholas von. "The Whig Milton, 1667–1700." In *Milton and Republicanism*, edited by David Armitage, Armand Himy, and Quentin Skinner, 229–253. Cambridge: Cambridge University Press, 1995.

Maltzahn, Nicholas von. "Milton, Marvell, and Toleration." In *Milton and Toleration*, edited by Sharon Achinstein and Elizabeth Sauer, 86–106. Oxford: Oxford University Press, 2007.

Mancini, Susanna, and Michel Rosenfeld, eds. *The Conscience Wars: Rethinking the Balance between Religion, Identity, and Equality.* Cambridge: Cambridge University Press, 2018.

Marshall, John. *John Locke, Toleration, and Early Enlightenment Culture.* Cambridge: Cambridge University Press, 2006.

McClure, Kirstie. "Difference, Diversity, and the Limits of Toleration." *Political Theory* 18, no. 3 (1990): 361–391.

McCrary, Charles. *Sincerely Held: American Religion, Secularism, and Belief.* Chicago: University of Chicago Press, 2022.

McIvor, Méadhbh. "Water in the Desert." *Anthropology News.* Accessed March 1, 2021. https://anthropology-news.org/index.php/2020/12/11/water-in-the-desert.

McQueen, Alison. *Political Realism in Apocalyptic Times.* Cambridge: Cambridge University Press, 2018.

Milton, John. *Complete Prose Works of John Milton, Volume 1–8.* Edited by Don Wolfe. New Haven, CT: Yale University Press, 1953–82.

Murphy, Andrew. *Conscience and Community: Revisiting Toleration and Religious Dissent in Early Modern England and America.* University Park, PN: Pennsylvania State University Press, 2001.

Murphy, Andrew. *Liberty, Conscience, and Toleration: The Political Thought of William Penn.* Oxford: Oxford University Press, 2015.

Myers, Benjamin. "'Following the Way Which Is Called Heresy': Milton and the Heretical Imperative." *Journal of the History of Ideas* 69, no. 3 (2008): 375–393.

Nadler, Steven. *Spinoza's Heresy: Immortality and the Jewish Mind.* Oxford: Oxford University Press, 2002.

NeJaime, Douglas, and Reva B. Siegel. "Conscience Wars: Complicity-Based Conscience Claims in Religion and Politics," *Yale Law Journal* 124, no. 7 (2015): 2516–2591.

Nussbaum, Martha. *Liberty of Conscience: In Defense of America's Tradition of Religious Equality.* New York: Basic Books, 2008.

BIBLIOGRAPHY 143

Obama, Barack. "Remarks in Hartford, Connecticut: 'A Politics of Conscience'" (Speech, Hartford, CT, June 23, 2007). *The American Presidency Project*, www.presidency.ucsb.edu/ws/?pid=76986.

Ojakangas, Mika. *The Voice of Conscience: A Political Genealogy of Western Ethical Experience*. New York: Bloomsbury, 2013.

Parkin, Jon. *Taming the Leviathan: The Reception of Thomas Hobbes's Political and Religious Ideas in England 1640–1700*. Cambridge: Cambridge University Press, 2007.

Patterson, Annabel. *Censorship and Interpretation: The Conditions of Writing and Reading in Early Modern England*. Madison, WI: University of Wisconsin Press, 1984.

Patterson, Annabel. *Early Modern Liberalism*. Cambridge: Cambridge University Press, 1997.

Patterson, Annabel. *Milton's Words*. Oxford: Oxford University Press, 2009.

Pear, Robert, and Jeremy W. Peters. "Trump Gives Health Workers New Religious Liberty Protections." *New York Times*. Accessed March 1, 2018. www .nytimes.com/2018/01/18/us/health-care-office-abortion-contraception.html.

Perkins, William. *William Perkins, 1558–1602, English Puritanist, His Pioneer Works on Casuistry: "A Discourse of Conscience" and "The Whole Treatise of Cases of Conscience"*. Edited by Thomas Merrill. Netherlands: Nieuwkoop and B. De Graaf, 1996.

Platt, Elizabeth Reiner, Katherine Franke, Kira Shepherd, and Lilia Hadjiivanova. "Whose Faith Matters? The Fight for Religious Liberty beyond the Christian Right." *Columbia Law School, Law, Rights, and Religion Project*. Accessed March 1, 2021. https://lawrightsreligion.law.columbia.edu/sites/default/ files/content/Images/Whose%20Faith%20Matters%20Full%20Report%20 12.12.19.pdf.

Ploof, Rebecca. "The Automaton, the Actor and the Sea Serpent: Leviathan and the Politics of Metaphor." *History of Political Thought* 39, no. 4 (2018): 634–661.

Popkin, Richard. *The History of Scepticism: From Savanarola to Bayle, Expanded Edition*. Oxford: Oxford University Press, 2003.

Qudrat, Maryam. "Confronting Jihad: A Defect in the Hobbesian Educational Strategy." In *Hobbes Today: Insights for the Twenty-First Century*, edited by S. A. Lloyd, 229–240. Cambridge: Cambridge University Press, 2012.

Rawls, John. *A Theory of Justice*. Cambridge, MA: Harvard University Press, 1971.

Rawls, John. *Political Liberalism: Expanded Edition*. New York: Columbia University Press, 2005.

Rogers, Melvin, and Jack Turner. *African American Political Thought: A Collected History*. Chicago: University of Chicago Press, 2021.

144 BIBLIOGRAPHY

Rosenthal, Michael. "Spinoza's Republican Argument for Toleration." *Journal of Political Philosophy* 11, no. 3 (2003): 320–337.

Runciman, David. *Political Hypocrisy: The Mask of Power, from Hobbes to Orwell and Beyond, Revised Edition*. Princeton: Princeton University Press, 2018.

Rutherford, Samuel. *A Free Disputation against Pretended Liberty of Conscience*. London: Printed by R.I. for Andrew Crook, 1649.

Ryan, Alan. "A More Tolerant Hobbes?" In *Justifying Toleration: Conceptual and Historical Perspectives*, edited by Susan Mendus, 37–60. Cambridge: Cambridge University Press, 1988.

Ryan, Alan. "Hobbes, Toleration, and the Inner Life." In *The Nature of Political Theory*, edited by David Miller and Larry Seidentop, 197–218. Oxford: Clarendon Press, 1983.

Sandel, Michael. "Religious Liberty: Freedom of Choice or Freedom of Conscience." In *Secularism and its Critics*, edited by Rajeev Bhargava, 85–92. Oxford: Oxford University Press, 1998.

Sauer, Elizabeth. *'Paper Contestations' and Textual Communities in England, 1640–1675*. Toronto: University of Toronto Press, 2005.

Sauer, Elizabeth. "Milton's *Of True Religion*, Protestant Nationhood, and the Negotiation of Liberty." *Milton Quarterly* 40, no. 1 (2006): 1–19.

Silver, Victoria. "Milton's Equitable Grounds of Toleration." In *Milton and Toleration*, edited by Sharon Achinstein and Elizabeth Sauer, 144–170. Oxford: Oxford University Press, 2007.

Skinner, Quentin. *Liberty before Liberalism*. Cambridge: Cambridge University Press, 1998.

Skinner, Quentin. *Vision of Politics, Volume 2*. Cambridge: Cambridge University Press, 2002.

Skinner, Quentin. *From Humanism to Hobbes: Studies in Rhetoric and Politics*. Cambridge: Cambridge University Press, 2018.

Smallenburg, Harry. "Government of the Spirit: Style, Structure and Theme in Treatise of Civil Power." In *Achievements of the Left Hand: Essays on the Prose of John Milton Achievements of the Left Hand*, edited by Michael Lieb and John Shawcross, 219–238. Amherst, MA: University of Massachusetts Press, 1974.

Smith, Nigel. *Is Milton Better than Shakespeare?* Cambridge, MA: Harvard University Press, 2008.

Smith, Steven. *Spinoza, Liberalism, and the Question of Jewish Identity*. New Haven, CT: Yale University Press, 1997.

Spinoza, Baruch. *The Collected Works of Spinoza, Volume 2*. Edited and translated by Edwin Curley. Princeton: Princeton University Press, 2016.

Spurr, John. "The Strongest Bond of Conscience: Oaths and the Limits of Tolerance in Early Modern England." In *Contexts of Conscience in Early Modern Europe, 1500–1700*, edited by Harald Braun and Edward Vallance, 151–165. New York: Palgrave Macmillan, 2004.

Steinberg, Justin. "Spinoza's Curious Defense of Toleration." In *Spinoza's 'Theological-Political Treatise': A Critical Guide*, edited by Yitzhak Melamed and Michael Rosenthal, 231–249. Cambridge: Cambridge University Press, 2010.

Stoll, Abraham. *Conscience in Early Modern English Literature, Volume 1*. Cambridge: Cambridge University Press, 2017.

Stout, Jeffrey. "Religion Unbound: Ideals and Powers from Cicero to King." Gifford Lecture Series, The University of Edinburgh, Edinburgh, UK, May 2, 2017.

Strohm, Paul. *Conscience: A Very Short Introduction*. Oxford: Oxford University Press, 2011.

Stutzman, Barronelle. "Why a Friend Is Suing Me: The Arlene's Flowers Story." *Seattle Times*. Accessed March 1, 2021. www.seattletimes.com/opinionwhy-a-good-friend-is-suing-me-the-arlenes-flowers-story.

Sullivan, Winnifred, Elizabeth Shakman Hurd, Saba Mahmood, and Peter Danchin, eds. *Politics of Religious Freedom*. Chicago: University of Chicago Press, 2015.

Sullivan, Winnifred. *The Impossibility of Religious Freedom*. Princeton: Princeton University Press, 2007.

Swaine, Lucas. "Freedom of Thought as a Basic Liberty." *Political Theory* 46, no. 3 (2018): 405–425.

Swaine, Lucas. *Liberal Conscience: Politics and Principle in a World of Religious Pluralism*. New York: Columbia University Press, 2006.

Targoff, Ramie. *Common Prayer: The Language of Public Devotion in Early Modern England*. Chicago: University of Chicago Press, 2001.

Taylor, Charles. *A Secular Age*. Cambridge, MA: Harvard University Press, 2007.

Thoreau, Henry David. *Thoreau: Political Writings*. Edited by Nancy Rosenblum. Cambridge: Cambridge University Press, 1996.

Thoreau, Henry David. *Thoreau: Collected Essays and Poems*. Edited by Elizabeth Hall Witherell. New York: Penguin, 2001.

Tralau, Johan. "Hobbes Contra Liberty of Conscience." *Political Theory* 39, no. 1 (2010): 58–84.

BIBLIOGRAPHY

Tuck, Richard. "Hobbes and Locke on Toleration." In *Thomas Hobbes and Political Theory*, edited by Mary Dietz, 153–171. Lawrence, KS: University of Kansas Press, 1990.

Tuck, Richard. "Hobbes, Conscience, and Christianity." In *The Oxford Handbook of Hobbes*, edited by Aloysius Patrick Martinich and Kinch Hoekstra, 579–601. Oxford: Oxford University, 2016.

Turchetti, Maria. "Religious Concord and Political Tolerance in Sixteenth- and Seventeenth-Century France." *The Sixteenth Century Journal* 22, no. 1 (1991): 15–25.

Uddin, Asma. *When Islam Is Not a Religion: Inside America's Fight for Religious Freedom*. New York: Pegasus Books, 2019.

Vaughan, Geoffrey. *Behemoth Teaches Leviathan: Thomas Hobbes on Political Education*. Lanham, MA: Lexington Books, 2002.

Vischer, Robert. *Conscience and the Common Good: Reclaiming the Space between Person and State*. Cambridge: Cambridge University Press, 2009.

Waldron, Jeremy. "Locke, Toleration and the Rationality of Persecution." In *Justifying Toleration: Conceptual and Historical Approaches*, edited by Susan Mendus, 61–86. Cambridge: Cambridge University Press, 1988.

Waldron, Jeremy. *God, Locke, and Equality*. Cambridge: Cambridge University Press, 2002.

Waldron, Jeremy. "Hobbes on Public Worship." In *Toleration and Its Limits*, edited by Jeremy Waldron and Melissa Williams, 31–53. New York: New York University Press, 2008.

Waldron, Jeremy. *The Harm in Hate Speech*. Cambridge, MA: Harvard University Press, 2012.

Walsham, Alexandra. "Ordeals of Conscience: Casuistry, Conformity and Confessional Identity in Post-Reformation England." In *Contexts of Conscience in Early Modern Europe, 1500–1700*, edited by Harald Braun and Edward Vallance, 32–48. New York: Palgrave Macmillan, 2004.

Walsham, Alexandra. *Charitable Hatred: Tolerance and Intolerance in England, 1500–1700*. Manchester: Manchester University Press, 2006.

Walzer, Michael. *Obligations: Essays on Disobedience, War, and Citizenship*. Cambridge, MA: Harvard University Press, 1970.

Walzer, Michael. *On Toleration*. New Haven, CT: Yale University Press, 2008.

Warren, Scott. "In Defense of Wilderness: Policing Public Borderlands," *South Atlantic Quarterly* 116, no. 4: 863–872.

Williams, Melissa, and Jeremy Waldron, eds. *Toleration and Its Limits*. New York: New York University Press, 2008.

Worden, Blair. *Literature and Politics in Cromwellian England: John Milton, Andrew Marvell, Marchamont Nedham.* Oxford: Oxford University Press, 2009.

Worden, Blair. *Roundhead Reputations: The English Civil War and the Passions of Posterity.* New York: Penguin, 2002.

Worden, Blair. *Literature and Politics in Cromwellian England: John Milton, Andrew Marvell, Marchamont Nedham.* Oxford: Oxford University Press, 2009.

Yovel, Yirmiyahu. *Spinoza and Other Heretics, The Marrano of Reason.* Princeton: Princeton University Press, 1992.

Yovel, Yirmiyahu. *The Other Within: The Marranos: Split Identity and Emerging Modernity.* Princeton: Princeton University Press, 2009.

Zagorin, Perez. *Ways of Lying: Dissimulation, Persecution and Conformity in Early Modern Europe.* Cambridge, MA: Harvard University Press, 1990.

Zagorin, Perez. *How the Idea of Religious Toleration Came to the West.* Princeton: Princeton University Press, 2003.

Zurbuchen, Simone. "Republicanism and Toleration." In *Republicanism: A Shared European Heritage, Volume 2,* edited by Quentin Skinner and Martin van Gelderen, 47–72. Cambridge: Cambridge University Press, 2002.

Index

African American political thought, 20
authenticity, 20, 111–114, 123–124
authority, ecclesiastical, 2, 16, 53, 75, 79
authority, political, 2, 16, 41, 88, 118

Bayle, Pierre, 8–10, 17–20, 34, 38, 90–107,
    109, 111–114, 122, 125–130, 134
    atheism, 85, 91
    Catholicism, 91, 100–102, 105
    difference, religious, 91–92, 102–103
    Dutch Republic, 91
    Edict of Nantes, 91
    heresy, 95–96, 99, 101, 104–106
    hypocritical conformity, 8, 10–12, 14–15,
      17–19, 91–112, 126–129
    Islam, 91–92, 105
    Judaism, 91–92
    liberty of conscience, 8–12, 14–21, 91–95,
      109–130
    Philosophical Commentary, 91–94, 101
    radicalization, 17, 91, 94, 104–106,
      126–127
    skepticism, 92–94
belief, religious, 1, 5–6, 14, 92, 95,
    120–121, 131

coercion, futility of, 13–15, 42, 52–54,
    73–74, 82, 94, 107
confessional society. *See* sectarianism,
    religious
conformity, 8, 10–11, 14–19, 22–26, 30–37,
    39–43, 45–46, 52–55, 61, 66–69, 71–79,
    81–114, 123–129, 133–134. *See also*
    hypocritical conformity
conscientious objection, 2, 88, 115–118
conventicles, 11

Davis, Kim, 3–4
democracy, American, 1, 19, 123–127, 132

disorder, civil, 18, 44, 49, 65, 72, 75, 88,
    102–103
dissenter, 6–8, 10–13, 15–19, 22, 24–26, 30–32,
    34–42, 44, 46, 48–49, 51, 55–56, 58–61,
    65, 68–71, 74, 76–78, 80–87, 89–101,
    103–107, 109–113, 118–121, 125–134
*Dobbs v. Jackson Women's Health
    Organization*, 4

early modernity, 6–7, 10–11, 19–22, 32,
    93–95, 108–113
education, civic, 9, 16, 44–46, 54–59, 61–68,
    110–111, 121–123, 133
Employment Division v. Smith, 119–120
equality, marriage, 4, 115–117, 119–121, 127
equality, racial, 2, 120

fanaticism, religious, 8, 104, 106. *See also*
    radicalization
First Amendment, 1
freedom, 1–5, 7–9, 12, 15–16, 18–27,
    30, 34–36, 39–49, 52, 68–83, 86–90,
    108–110, 114, 118–119, 123–124,
    128–131, 136
    of expression, 18, 27, 32, 35–36, 39, 69,
      72, 74, 76, 79, 80–83, 85–87, 89–91, 108,
      110, 123, 126, 129–131, 136
    inward, 16, 19, 25, 35–36, 39, 42–43,
      45–49, 71–72, 80, 119
    outward, 25, 35–36, 39, 72, 81, 130
    of press, 21, 25–27, 36
    of speech, 5, 72, 80, 81, 84
freedom, religious, 1, 4, 18–19, 108, 114,
    130–131

heresy, 25, 31–33, 38, 76, 95–96, 99, 101,
    104–106
heterodoxy, religious, 1, 26, 31–33, 42–44,
    55–56, 88, 96, 99–100, 106

Hobbes, Thomas, 8–10, 16–19, 34, 40–75,
   77, 79, 88, 101–104, 109–114, 118–123,
   129–133
   ambition, 66–67
   authority, ecclesiastical, 2, 53, 79
   Behemoth, 43, 45, 60, 63, 65
   casuistry, 49–50
   coercion, futility of, 42, 52–53
   De Cive, 41, 44, 47, 50, 60, 63
   disobedience, 2, 49, 52, 55, 57, 88–89
   divine inspiration, 59
   English Civil War, 63, 65
   Erastianism, 43, 52, 79, 119
   hypocritical conformity, 8, 10, 15, 40–45,
      54–56, 61, 66–68, 77, 108–110
   Leviathan, 13, 41, 43–45, 47–49, 51–53,
      55–56, 58, 60–61, 63–65
   liberty of conscience, 8–12, 14–16, 18–21,
      40, 41–46, 49–54, 56–58, 62, 68–69,
      109–111, 114, 118–120
   miracles, 52
   nature, state of, 41, 103
   opinion, 16, 44, 46, 48–51, 54–59, 61–67,
      115, 121
   peace, 16, 40–41, 44, 47, 55–56, 61–68, 121
   prophecy, 59
   sectarianism, religious, 42, 75, 102
   shared knowledge, 47–49
   sovereignty, 16–17, 43–45, 51–58, 61–65,
      68–70, 121
   sovereignty, competing, 55, 58, 62, 65
   sovereignty, divided, 55
   witnesses, 47–48
house chapels, 11
hypocrisy. *See* hypocritical conformity
hypocritical conformity, 8, 10–11, 15–19,
   23–24, 32–43, 56, 61, 70, 74, 77–78,
   83–85, 90, 92, 95, 98–101, 103, 107,
   109–112, 126, 129, 135

immigration, 2, 113, 132–134
Islam, 5–6, 69, 91, 105, 108, 125, 135–136

L.G.B.T.Q.I.A.+ rights, 3–4, 116–118
law, anti-discrimination, 3–4, 116–117,
   122–129
liberty of conscience, 1–19, 21–27, 32–36,
   38–42, 44–46, 49–54, 56–58, 62–74,
   79–81, 90–91, 95, 108–114, 117–121,
   123–125, 129–136
Locke, John, 13–14, 24, 45, 52, 73, 85

*Masterpiece Cakeshop v. Colorado Civil
   Rights Commission*, 3–4, 114, 117
Milton, John, 1–2, 5–6, 8–10, 15–16, 18–42,
   56, 60–61, 64, 72, 74–76, 81, 109–110,
   112–114, 117–119, 130–136
   Areopagitica, 21–22, 24, 27, 33, 36,
      57
   book licensing, 22–25, 27–31, 33,
      36, 39
   books, 21, 22–25, 27–31, 33, 36, 39
   capacity of reason, 24, 30, 31, 35–36
   Catholicism, 6, 23–24, 33
   coercion, futility of, 30
   evil, 24, 27–30, 39
   heresy, 25, 31–33, 38, 76
   hypocritical conformity, 8, 10, 12, 14–15,
      18, 22–24, 26, 32–40, 42, 74, 108–110,
      112–113, 129
   intellectual discourse, 25
   Judaism, 23
   liberty of conscience, 1–2, 5–6, 8–12,
      14–21, 22–27, 32–36, 38–42, 44–46,
      109–110, 114, 117–118, 132
   Popery, 24
   religious uniformity, 23, 34, 37
   religious unity, 23
   republicanism, 26
   *A Treatise of Civil Power in Ecclesiastical
      Causes*, 24

Newman v. Piggie, 120
No More Deaths, 131–132, 135

Obergefell v. Hodges, 3, 115

peace, political, 16, 40–41, 46, 55–56, 61–63,
   65, 68, 75–76, 102, 122
persecution, religious, 7, 10–13, 17, 20,
   22–24, 26, 35–38, 40–42, 68, 69, 77,
   89–91, 94–96, 101, 105–107
persuasion, inward, 24, 39, 42–44, 61,
   67, 72, 77, 80, 82–83, 85, 89, 95, 101,
   107
Phillips, Jack, 3, 117, 135
pluralism, 5–6, 11, 43, 74, 78–79, 82,
   102–103, 108, 114, 122

radicalization, 17, 51, 76, 94, 105, 122,
   127–128
religion, majoritarian, 108
religion, minoritarian, 108–109, 114, 125

150 INDEX

religious dissimulation. *See* hypocritical
  conformity
reproductive justice, 4, 118, 128–129

sectarianism, religious, 22–23, 31–34, 38–39,
  42, 75, 95, 102–103
sincerity, 17, 20, 37, 73, 84, 88, 97, 123
social contract, 50–51
sovereignty, 16–17, 43, 45, 51–52, 54–55,
  58, 61–65, 68–71, 74–75, 79–80, 86–87,
  90–91, 121
Spinoza, Baruch, 8–10, 16–18, 20, 24, 68–92,
  102, 103, 109, 111–112, 114, 122–126,
  129, 130, 133–134
  authority, ecclesiastical, 2, 75, 79
  baptism, 70
  Catholicism, 70, 77, 85
  civic trust, 8, 17, 68, 72, 84, 89–90, 111,
    133–134
  coercion, futility of, 73–74, 82
  difference, religious, 8, 71, 75, 78
  Erastianism, 75
  freedom, 8, 12, 68–69, 71–77, 79–83,
    86–87, 89–90, 130, 136
  hypocritical conformity, 8, 10, 15–17,
    68–78, 81–91, 108–111, 123
  irrationality, 76
  Islam, 69, 125
  Japan, 77–80

Judaism, 5, 6, 70
liberty of conscience, 8–12, 14–15, 17–19,
  21, 68–69, 71–74, 79–81, 90, 109, 111,
  114–125, 133
Locke, 14, 85
Marranos, Portuguese, 69
  prejudice, 76, 130
  religious assimilation, 70
  sincerity, 17, 20, 73, 84, 88, 123
  Theological-Political Treatise, 69–73
stability, political, 9, 16–17, 27, 40–41,
  51–52, 55–57, 61–63, 67–68, 70–71, 75,
  79–80, 84, 87, 90–91, 102, 111, 118
state of nature, 41, 75, 77, 103

toleration, religious, 3, 5, 7–10, 12–15,
  18, 23, 25, 33, 38, 42, 45–46, 49–50,
  68–69, 72–73, 83–86, 88, 91–94, 96, 99,
  101–102, 107, 109, 112, 118, 123, 125,
  127, 130, 135
trust, civic, 8, 17, 68, 72–73, 84, 89, 111,
  123, 133–134

United States v. Warren, 130–135

worship, mandatory, 11, 19, 38, 92
worship, religious, 6, 11, 32, 37–39, 45,
  49, 70, 76–77, 80, 91, 95, 105, 108,
  110, 121

Printed in the United States
by Baker & Taylor Publisher Services